The Castles

of

County Limerick

The Castles
of
County Limerick

Michael J Carroll

Bantry Studio Publications

ACKNOWLEDGEMENTS

I wish to acknowledge all the authors of many generations whose work I consulted in preparing this volume. My main references are listed individually elsewhere. Particular thanks to Dick Richards for research and administrative assistance. Pat O'Brien of Celtic Bookshop in Limerick was a great help in the acquisition of source documents.

Text © 2005 Michael J Carroll

Published by Michael J Carroll, Bantry Co Cork. Ireland

First published in 2005

A Bantry Studio Publications paperback 2005

bantrydesigns@iol.ie

All rights reserved. No part of this publication may be reproduced, stored in a retrieval system or transmitted in any form or by any means, electronic, mechanical, photocopying, recording or otherwise without prior permission of the author and publisher.

This book is sold subject to the condition that it shall not, by way of trade or otherwise, be lent, re-sold, hired out or otherwise circulated without the publisher's prior consent in any form of binding or cover other than that in which it is published and without a similar condition including this condition being imposed on a subsequent purchaser.

British Library Cataloguing in Publication Date
Michael John Carroll

The Castles of County Limerick
Ireland: Local History. Irish History

ISBN: 0 9519415 9 3

Cover and illustrations by Alan Langford of Southampton, UK
Printed in Spain by GraphyCems

Contents

Preface	13
Introduction	16
Abington / Woney / Butler's Castle	57
Adare Castle	58
Amigan (Amogan) Castle	62
Ardpatrick Castle	63
Askeaton Castle	63
Athlacca Castle	72
Aughanish Castle	72
Baggotstown Castle	73
Ballinard (Ballynard) Castle	74
Ballingarry Castle	75
Ballyallinan Castle	78
Ballybricken Castle / Old Court Castle	79
Ballycahane Castle	79
Ballyclogh (Knocknagaul) Castle 1	80
Ballyclogh Castle 2	80
Ballyculhaun (Ballyculhane) Castle	81
Ballycullen Castle	82
Ballyegan Castle / Castle Egney	83
Ballyegnybeg Castle	84
Ballyengland Castle	84
Ballygleaghan Castle	84
Ballygrennan Castle 1	85
Ballygrennan (Ballygenan) Castle 2	86

Ballygubba Castle	86
Ballyguileataggle Castle	88
Ballymacshaneboy Castle	88
Ballynagarde Castle	89
Ballynahinch (Ballinahinch) Castle	89
Ballynamona Castle	90
Ballynoe Castle 1	90
Ballynoe Castle 2	91
Ballysheedy Castle / Tower House	92
Ballysiward (Howardstown) Castle	92
Ballysteen Castle	93
Ballytrasna (Bullytarsna) Castle	93
Ballyvoghan Castle	94
Ballyvorneen Castle	94
Ballywilliam Castle	95
Beagh Castle	95
Black Castle 1	98
Black Castle 2	103
Bolane Castle / Beolaun Castle	103
Bouchier's Castle	104
Brickfield (Kilbigly) Castle	106
Brittas Castle	106
Broghill Castle	107
Bruff Castle	108
Bruree (Upper Lotteragh) Castle	108
Bruree (Lower Lotteragh) Castle	109
Bulgaden Castle	114
Cahernarry Castle	114

Caherconlish Castle	114
Caherelly Old Castle	115
Cappagh Castle	116
Carrickania / Carraig an Fhiaigh Castle	117
Carrick-Kital Castle	118
Carrigareely Castle	118
Carrigogunnel Castle	118
Castle Comfort	123
Castleconnell Castle	123
Castle Oliver	127
Castle Erkin	128
Castlequarter Old Castle	128
Castle Rag	128
Castle Roberts	129
Castle Siward (Rathsiward)	129
Castle Troy	129
Castle Guard	130
Castlejane	131
Castlemahon (Mahoonagh) Castle	131
Castlematrix / Castle Matras	133
Castletown Castle 1	137
Castletown Castle 2	139
Castletown Castle 3	140
Cleanlis Castle / Castle Engliash	141
Cloghacloka Castle	141
Clogh Castle	142
Cloughkeating Castle	142
Clonshire (Cloonsheer) Castle	143

Cluggin Castle (Castle Cluggin)	143
Corgrig Castle	144
Corrin Castle	146
Courtbrown Castle	146
Court Castle	146
Crecora Castle / Ballinveala Castle	147
Creggane Castle	147
Croagh Castle	148
Croom Castle	148
Cullam Castle	150
Derreen Castle	151
Derryknockane Castle	152
Donaman (Dunnaman) Castle	152
Doon Castle	153
Doondonnell Castle	154
Drombanny Castle	154
Drumkeen House	155
Dunmoylan Castle	155
Dysert (Disert) Castle	157
Esclon (Esclone) Castle	159
Fanningstown Castle	161
Fantstown Castle	161
Fedamore Castle	162
Finnitterstown Castle	163
Garraunboy Castle	163
Garryfine Castle	164
Glebe Castle	164
Glenogra Castle	165

Glenquin (Glinquin) Castle	166
Glenstal Castle	168
Glin Castle	171
Gormanstown Castle	174
Gortadrumma Castle	174
Gurtnetubber (Gort-na-Tiobrad) Castle	175
Grange Castle	176
Greenaun Castle	177
Hospital Castle or Manor House	177
Killballyowen Castle	179
Kilbehenny Castle / Kilcolman Castle	179
Kilcosgrave (Killcosgriff) Castle	180
Kilcullane (Kilkillaun) Castle	180
Kilduff Castle	181
Kilfinny (Killfenny) Castle	182
Kilfinane Castle	183
Killanahan Castle	184
Killeedy Castle	184
Kilmacow Castle	185
Kilmallock Castle	186
Kilpeacon Castle	188
Knockainy Castle	189
Knockatancashlane Castle	190
Knocklong Castle	190
Leagaun/Liagan (Tobernea) Castle	191
Lickadoon (Lickadoen) Castle	192
Limerick City	193
John's Castle	193

Lissamota Castle	198
Lismakeery Castle	198
Lisnacullia (Lisnacullin) Castle	199
Longford Castle / Ballyneety Castle	200
Loghill (Loughill) Castle	202
Lower Shanid Castle	202
Luddenmore Castle	205
Maidstown (Baile Ui Bhenog) Castle	205
Millmount Castle	206
Milltown Castle	206
Morgans Castle	207
Mungret Castle	208
Newcastle (West) Castle 1	209
Newcastle Castle 2	212
Nicker Castle	213
Oola/Ulla Castle	213
Palacegrean (Pallas Grean) Castle	214
Pallaskenry Castle / Shanpallas Castle	215
Port (Portanard) Castle	216
Pullagh Castle	217
Raheen Castle / Cahervally Castle	219
Rath Castle	219
Rathcannon Castle	220
Rathgonin Castle	220
Rathkeale Castle	221
Rathmore Castle	221
Rathnaseer (Rath Na Saor) Castle	222
Rathurd Castle	223

Rawleystown (Raleighstown) Castle	223
Robertstown Castle	224
Rockbarton Castle	225
Rockstown (Rochestown) Castle	225
Ryves Castle	226
Shanid Castle	227
Skehacreggaun Castle	231
Skool (School) Castle	231
Stephenson (Stephenstown) Castle	232
Stoneville Castle	232
Tankerdstown Castle	233
Thomastown Castle	234
Tomdeely Castle	234
Tooreen Castle	236
Tullabracky Castle	236
Tullerboy Castle / Castle Ivers	237
Tullovin Castle	237
Williamstown Castle	237
Woodstock Castle / Bonistoe Castle	238
Index of alternative names	240
Bibliography	242

Preface

Castles present an irresistible force of attraction to both young and old. These ancient strongholds of the Anglo-Normans and Irish chieftains where dwelt many an important family now long gone are a reminder of an era when lavish parties were held, when battles were fought, sieges conducted, and when the thunder of cannons, shouts of battle and cries of the injured pervaded the deep walls. One can almost hear them now looking at the breaches, ruins and fallen walls.

Almost all of the castles suffered a barrage of cannon fire, pillage, and the flames of destruction. As some of the major castles had large halls within their outer protective walls with only thatched roofs these suffered from the fire arrows of the besiegers and were mostly destroyed or gutted. Most were rebuilt and repaired again and again but suffered the same fate during the Cromwellian conquest. Now only the ghosts of those slain in battle or murdered inhabit these old vaults which gives one the impression that they keep a silent vigil amidst the ruins and destroyed structures where they met their death.

The landscape of Limerick County is dotted with the ruins of many castles. As one drives along the main roads or byways some ruin or another comes into view in the distance. In locations like Bruree there were Anglo-Norman castles about every square mile protecting the territory of the various branches of De Lacy families. The castles vary in size from large imposing structures either of square or rectangular plan to smaller watch towers. Some were constructed with bawn and outer defensive walls with or without turrets at each corner while others were fortified tower houses or plain towers where garrisons were placed.

It is reputed that there were some four hundred and five castles in Limerick city and county. However, the historians Lenihane and Dowd only refer to about one hundred and twenty. Taking into consideration the area of Limerick County we previously accepted that the later figure was more accurate but this assumption now seems incorrect and I have entries for one hundred and eighty five identified castles. Some of the castles mentioned in this publication had name changes over the centuries depending on who was in occupation. I have corrected and amended these where historical fact indicates.

A large majority of the minor castles and tower houses have vanished off the landscape of County Limerick and only vague references as to their original location exist today. Little is known about many of these castles but they still deserve mention in this work solely to inform the reader that they did actually exist and can be used as reference for the archives or other historians.

On the other hand, many of the important castles and tower houses such as Askeaton, Adare, Croom, Carrigogunnel and Shannid are worthy of a book, in their own right. As in my previous publications on 'The Castles and Fortified Houses of West Cork' and 'The Castles of the Kingdom of Kerry' I have limited the space taken on the most important castles so as to accommodate what information has been gathered on the lesser known castles. In all, nearly 200 castles and tower houses have come up in research yet I do not claim that my list is definitive. Once this volume is in print there may be others to add to future editions.

Some of the finest castles and tower houses in Ireland were built in Limerick County mainly due to the Anglo-Norman influence in the region. Some of them, if still in a reasonably good state of repair would compare with the best of Norman architecture in the British Isles. With only the major stronghold of Limerick to protect their interest, the Anglo-Normans, who had gained land in the country by conquest, built many castles as strongholds. In fact, in some parishes there are a number of castles mainly occupied by branches of the same Anglo-Norman family, like the De Lacys of Bruree.

Contrary to what one might think, it was not the Irish who destroyed most of the castles but the Cromwellian and Williamite forces fighting against the Anglo-Normans and the remaining Irish Clans during the period of the Desmond rebellions.

As in my previous writing on Irish history, I sometimes disagree with the findings or statements of the Irish Annals or some of the noted historians and put forward some of my own views based on other sources. I especially refer to the role of the Knights Templar in Limerick County and elsewhere in Ireland. Whether any reference or history of their time in Ireland was purposely obliterated, following the suppression of the Order by Pope Clement V in 1312 A.D., is open to question. Most of the history of the period concerned was written by monks or by eminent Catholic historians like Rev. S.J. Keating, etc. You, the reader, can come to your own conclusions when you have read this book.

Introduction

Following the pattern established in the other books of this series, I shall relate a short history of Limerick County so that readers can acquaint themselves with the different phases of history of that county and the era of castle building can be better understood.

Due to the influence of the Vikings (Norsemen) in establishing a settlement on the island, which later constituted the fortress of John's Castle, I am obliged to commence with them in this historical account. Many historians refer to the Danes in the conquest of the western seaboard of Ireland, including Limerick and the surrounding area. In fact, these Vikings were not Danes but a mixture of Norwegians and Swedes, who were related to, or allies of, the Danes who came down the east coast of Ireland. The dividing line of their respective conquests was Dursey Island off the Beara Peninsula.

The Vikings first appeared on the Shannon in A.D. 795 and proceeded up the river to Luimneach where they pulled their boats ashore on what became known as King's Island. Having established themselves in a timber fortified fort adjacent to the river they began to plunder inland. After gainful expeditions inland where they gathered much booty, they departed so as to reach their homeland before the winter gales set in. But they were to be back the following summer in greater numbers with their shallow draft boats, which could navigate up most of the rivers of Ireland. Even when they encountered rapids or waterfalls they resorted to manhandling their boats overland until they gained smooth water again.

Luimneach became their main base and the centre of their operations on the west coast of Ireland, while the Irish tribes argued and fought amongst themselves. Some tribes even formed alliances with the Vikings to fight against their neighbours in their quest to gain further territory. At this stage some of the local tribes, fearing the inroads that the Norsemen were making into their own territories, prepared themselves for battle, and in A.D. 834 the O'Donovans engaged the enemy and defeated them with great losses.

The native tribes of Kerry joining together at about the same time defeated the Norsemen in a sea battle and another on land. This heralded the general native uprising against the northern invaders. The tribes of Connaught expelled many of them from their territories and the King of Cashel, Cormac MacCuilennan, forced them out of his kingdom. He and his chiefs were later killed in battle and, after this, the Norsemen became stronger and even ventured up the Shannon in A.D. 920 when they sacked Clonmacnois and Lough Derg and later ventured north to Lough Corrib.

Next, reinforced by many of their countrymen and also by Danes, their forces, under Amlav, defeated the local clans in 931 and went on to sack Galway. Their first major defeat happened in A.D. 942, when the Norsemen, under Tomar, were defeated by the combined forces of Connaught and those of the east coast. It is reputed that over four thousand of the enemy fell. In A.D. 945 the Irish Clans, under Callaghan, King of Cashel, marched on Luimneach and engaged the Norsemen in battle outside the fortifications at a place known as Singland. Only after their leaders were killed in single combat did the Norsemen retreat to the protection of their fort. The Irish followed and killed many thousands before burning the fortification to the ground. Thus began the temporary decline of the power of the Norsemen until they were reinforced from the homeland and then built their fortified base on Scattery Island. Brian Boru attacked this fortress killing their leader, Ivar, and his son. Many other battles were fought until the power of the men from the north was finally broken, namely, at the Battle of Clontarf, where Brian himself was killed.

Finally subdued, the Norsemen and the Danes with their families continued integrating with the Irish until they became like the Irish themselves. But, on the Irish side following the death of Brian Boru and his strong leadership, his surviving sons, Teige and Donagh, fought each other for kingship over the following years, until Turlogh, Teige's son, defeated his uncle Donagh, who retired to a monastery to see his last days out. Turlogh was succeeded by his son, Murtagh, who died in 1119, and with him the power of the rulers over the south of Ireland. The O'Briens were left with only Thomond, while in all other parts of Munster the local clans returned to their old ways – waging war on each other. Meanwhile, another strong invasion force was landing on the east coast which would rule Ireland for the following eight hundred years.

An event took place, in what we know today as Leinster, that changed the course of Irish history in the twelfth century. The young wife of Teigernan O'Rourke of Brefney left her husband and sought refuge and solace with Dearmuid Mac Murrogh, the King of Leinster. O'Rourke sought the assistance of Roderick O'Connor, King of Ireland, to get back his wife. Roderick raised an army and marched into

Leinster where he defeated Mac Murrogh, who was forced to place his charge in the protection of a nunnery and flee the country.

Having being received by King Henry of England, who happened to be waging war in France, he was promised assistance and told to go to Wales to meet the Viceroy, Ralph Griffin. After being promised assistance from a Robert Fitzstephens and his cousins, Maurice Fitzgerald and de Carraun (Carew), he returned to Ireland incognito, after pledging his daughter, Aoife, and the town of Wexford to Fitzgilbert, the Earl of Pembroke – son of Gilbert de Clare 'Strongbow'.

Fitzstephens with some other knights arrived the following summer accompanied by some three hundred professional soldiers, who happened to be Welsh mercenaries. They landed near Wexford and immediately were joined by Dearmuid with five hundred horses. He granted the town of Wexford to Fitzstephens and a tract of land to another knight called Harmon Morty who was an emissary of Strongbow. Now, with his numbers increased to about three thousand, Dearmuid marched north into Ossory. Donough, the King of Leinster sued for peace while Roderick O'Connor, the King of Ireland, marched east with a large army but was unable to engage Dearmuid in battle as he and his force took to the woods and forests. Eventually, a peace was arranged whereby Dearmuid would get back his kingdom on the condition that the Anglo-Normans returned to Britain. This condition was never fulfilled.

The following summer Fitzgerald arrived, again near Wexford, with a small army made up of knights in armour, footsoldiers and bowmen. Dearmuid immediately marched his army to join him and in so doing broke the peace agreed with Roderick the previous year. The combined forces then marched to Dublin, which immediately surrendered. Now filled with ambition to become the King of Ireland, Dearmuid waited for Maurice Fitzgerald to arrive with more men. Meanwhile, the Earl of Strangwell sent Redmond de la Grose and William Fitzgerald to Ireland with a small force. These were immediately attacked by the King of the Decies (Waterford) but the Irish force was defeated in a bloody battle.

The day following this encounter, St. Bartholomew's Day 1170, Strongbow himself arrived in Ireland with over two hundred knights in armour, a thousand bowmen and about two thousand five hundred trained footsoldiers. This was a sizeable invasion force and, having been joined by Dearmuid's army, they both marched on Waterford, which they captured after a dire struggle with much bloodshed. Strongbow and Aoifa were married in the Ostman church of the Holy Trinity. Now with the submission of Waterford they then marched to Dublin and, while the inhabitants were trying to negotiate a peaceful surrender, the north wall was breached and what followed was a massacre of most of the inhabitants.

Meanwhile, in Munster the local clans continued with their inter-tribal warfare, in their quest to gain territory instead of viewing the danger presented by the new invaders, who were far more formidable than the Danes and Vikings. The knights, dressed in their glittering armour with their long spears, the bowmen with their bows and crossbows, the footsoldiers in their battle formation and the well-organized tactics against any enemy should have alerted the clans to the impending danger. But, as in the past, the country lacked a strong leader who could bring all the clans together.

Amongst those Anglo-Normans who came to Ireland was

Maurice Fitzgerald, also known as Maurice the Invader, who landed at Bannow Strand, near Wexford c. 1169. He was the son of Gerald of Windsor and Nesta an Ryse, who was daughter of Ap Ryse, Prince of Wales. He established himself in Leinster. His son, Gerald established the Kildare branch of the Geraldines while his other son, Thomas, was granted lands around Shanid by Hamo de Valognes. Here at Shanid he erected his stronghold and tried to dominate the other Anglo-Normans and the rest of Munster.

Fearing that Strongbow would claim the country for himself, Henry II landed in Waterford in 1172 with a strong army which vastly outnumbered Strongbow's force. Assured of Strongbow's loyalty Henry had little to do except receive the homage and submission of a number of native clan chieftains. Amongst the first to arrive was Donald O'Brien, who surrendered the city of Limerick to Henry and agreed to hold the city and his kingdom as a fief of the English king. No sooner had the English king departed when Donald renounced his allegiance and drove the English out of Limerick.

Fearful of the uprising, Strongbow marched from Dublin and was met near Thurles by Donald and his Dalcassian soldiers. In the ensuing surprise attack at night, Donald was victorious and Strongbow was obliged to retreat to Dublin. Availing of the opportunity of having a large army, Donal laid waste the territories of those minor clans of Munster who had not come to his aid. These included the MacCarthys, O'Sullivans and O'Donoghues, who were obliged to move south into Cork and Kerry during the following years. Meanwhile, Henry granted Limerick to Philip de Braose, a knight of Brecknock, and it was soon occupied by an Anglo-Norman force. The O'Briens later overcame these and the fortification reverted to Irish hands.

In 1175, Raymond le Gros was sent with an army to recover the city of Limerick. Crossing the river in flood with only minor loss of life the city was taken amidst great slaughter. Sometime later, the Irish laid siege to Limerick, and Raymond, being in Dublin, was summoned to march south with the Anglo-Norman army. He was met by Donald with his forces near Cashel who suffered great losses in the ensuing battle. Donald surrendered to Raymond and again pledged his allegiance to the Crown. With the death of Strongbow, Raymond was recalled to Dublin and, seizing the opportunity, Donald torched the city of Limerick so that it would no longer be a stronghold for the English.

Seeing that he was losing power in Ireland, King Henry sent John, his son, as Chief Governor to Ireland accompanied by a large army and a host of adventurers intending to enrich themselves. The Irish chieftains who came to pay homage were amazed at the young Prince's attitude and the unruly behavior of those who tagged around him, and soon departed. When they arrived back at their territories they prepared to revolt but instead began once more to wage war on each other.

When Donald O'Brien died in 1194 Munster became a leaderless province and the English regained Limerick. On his accession to the crown, John gave the custody of Limerick to William de Burgo and the rule of the O'Briens ended with the charter of 1197. This began with the expulsion from these territories of other native tribes, including the O'Donovans, and a part of the O'Mahony clan, who moved from the north of the county near the Galtee Mountains into County Cork. In 1197/8 Hamo de Voloignes, the chief Justice of the Crown in Ireland, was granted large tracts of land from the Shannon to Bruree by King John. Some years later, Hamo de Voloignes gave Bruree to John de Mareys (de

Marisco) whom his daughter, Mabel, had married. Bruree and its lands were handed down to Maurice de Lesse (De Lacy) through a later marriage. William de Burgh received all the lands west of those of Hamo de Valoignes. These lands of de Burgh later became the possessions of the Fitzgeralds, or Geraldines. Sir Thomas de Botiller (Butler) also came into possession of lands in east Limerick, as well as de Cogans, de Penrys, Tankars, de Lecton (Liston), de Goulys (Gould), Russell and Dundon, while the territory of part of west Limerick and north Kerry came to the sons of Maurice Fitzgerald. King John also granted lands to Meiler Fitzhenry. The following years saw the O'Briens and the Anglo-Normans consolidating their positions in County Limerick, and even as far as Cork and Kerry, displacing any minor clans who were in these regions.

After the visit of King John c. 1210 the spoils of Munster were divided amongst his favorite knights and during his stay in Limerick he ordered that a stone castle be built which still bears his name. With Limerick as a stronghold of the conquerors, many English came across the water and settled in the city. Following his example, the major Anglo-Norman families began to claim their lands and to build castles for their protection. In the short period of some ten years, the Anglo-Norman families built over a hundred stone castles in County Limerick. In fact, by 1223, Limerick and Kerry were Anglo-Norman or Anglo-Irish counties through intermarriage. In November 1259, John Fitzthomas received from Prince Edward a grant in fee of the Desmond territory or kingdom.

Mention has to be made at this stage of the Knights Templar. Being related to, or friends of, those who had come to Ireland, the Templars, taking advantage of the situation, moved to Ireland in substantial numbers feeling that their position in England and France was under threat, both from Rome as well as the English and French Monarchies. It is not known how many came in those first decades of Anglo-Norman occupation but from the number of castles and churches they built in those early stages it can be surmised that at least five hundred of this powerful semi-religious order did arrive. When we remember that the Templars had amassed great wealth and were considered the bankers of Europe, as well as controlling the price of the harvest of various countries, it may seem strange that they came to Ireland, which was the last outpost of the continent of Europe. As the Templars were reputed to be the guardians of the Holy Grail and possibly The Ark of the Covenant, what were they doing in Ireland? Also, why did they build their extraordinary castles and adjoining churches and preceptories? I will try to answer these questions in a future publication.

With most of Limerick County under their control, the Anglo-Normans began to fortify their possessions by building stone castles in suitable defensive locations on their newly gained territories, replacing the old motte and bailey structures. The massive stone castles were for both protection and as a sign of the strength of the owner. Not satisfied with their gains in Limerick, the Anglo-Normans under Meiler moved along the coast into north Kerry. About this time, Geoffrey de Marisco married the Irish widow of Thomas Fitzgerald's brother and in so doing took possession of a large part of Kerry which was not already in Anglo-Norman hands.

Having felt the brunt of the Anglo-Norman knights, archers and professional soldiery, the Irish chieftains sought the assistance of Scottish mercenaries from the outer islands and the Hebrides, who were part Irish and Norse. They fought in the military formation of the Vikings in heavy mail and with long two-headed axes. They became known as the 'gallowglass' and they became an integral part of each Irish chieftain's army.

In 1254, Henry III granted to his young son, Edward, the Lordship of Ireland. The king had hoped that young Edward would come to Ireland to rule but this did not happen due to minor uprisings in England. Instead the Anglo-Normans, who were already amassing territory and wealth, were granted more privileges and power by Edward.

Things changed when Finghin MacCarthy of County Cork came to power after the murder of his father by one of the Anglo-Normans. Gathering all his forces and those of his allies he drove the Anglo-Normans out of West Cork. After the decisive battle against the Anglo-Normans at Callan, in 1261, where many knights of the Fitzgeralds were killed, including John Fitzthomas and his son, he continued into Kerry and to the borders of Limerick, capturing each enemy castle one after the other, including the stronghold of Shanid. In fact, he presented the greatest threat to the Anglo-Normans in Munster since their arrival. However, when Finghin met his death at Ringarone Castle near Kinsale, in County Cork, the Anglo-Normans began to regain most of their castles and lands and their colonization of Limerick, Kerry and Cork continued in earnest.

By the middle of the fourteenth century most of southern Munster was in the hands of the Geraldines. John Fitzthomas, who died at Callan, was succeeded by his grandson, Thomas, who built a stone castle at Shanid c. 1285. Shanid became the chief seat of the Geraldines until they moved to Askeaton during the War of Roses (1455 to 1485).

When Edward Bruce came to Ireland in 1316 there was a minor uprising and Limerick again fell into Irish hands.

Edward came to Limerick and stayed for about six months, hoping that he would be accepted by the Irish and Anglo-Normans as their king. He marched his army around Ireland seeking assistance but unfortunately, due to the lack of food, he laid waste much of the country, including the lands of the Butlers and the Fitzgeralds. He was crowned King of Ireland in Dundalk in 1317. In that same year, Sir Roger Mortimer, who was an able tactician in warfare, arrived in Youghal and moved northwards to Dublin. He sent an army led by John de Bermingham, who marched north to engage Edward and his Irish allies in battle. This was no contest and Edward and his forces were utterly defeated. Edward died of his wounds on the battlefield while his decimated Irish force, including the O'Briens and many other southern tribes, returned home.

For the next two hundred and fifty years, the Geraldines (Fitzgeralds) held almost complete sway over Munster and most of Leinster, except Dublin. They became a power unto themselves, replacing the old Irish kings of the various regions and ruling like princes.

The Tudor monarchs of England were aware of the threat of the Geraldines to their influence in Ireland and began to try to establish a central government in Dublin. This soon came to the notice of the Geraldines who were against the granting of lands by the Crown to more English colonists and adventurers.

In 1316 the Geraldines and the MacCarthys joined forces and drove the earlier English colonists and settlers out of parts of Limerick and Kerry. In an argument over territory Diarmuid MacCarthy was murdered in Tralee by William Fitzmaurice and his aides. Maurice Fitzgerald, who was the head of the Geraldines at this time, gave orders that William be blinded as punishment. William and his associates were hanged later as Maurice consolidated his position. By the 1320s, the native tribes began to reclaim their territories where possible, as the era of confiscation and land-exploitation was coming to a temporary end. The Anglo-Normans or Anglo-Irish were now content to rule with their Irish counterparts so they commenced building their fortified houses to rule over their lands.

When Edward II was deposed, and England was under Regency Rule of the Queen Mother, Maurice was created Earl of Desmond (1329), which was to the benefit of all his relations and allies amongst the native Irish. But when Edward III came to the English throne, Maurice lost his title and was confined to jail at Dublin Castle. On his release, two years later, he was reinstated to his former title of Earl and returned south. He was then, together with the Earl of Ormond, requested by the young King to send an army to Scotland to assist the English but they got little thanks for their efforts and losses.

Later, when the King appointed a Sir John Morice, who was just a knight, deputy in Ireland, he summoned a parliament of all Ireland for Dublin in October 1341. The Earl of Desmond and the Earl of Kildare summoned a rival parliament in Kilkenny for November, where they decided to send envoys direct to the King stating that the corruption of the King's ministers in Ireland had brought Ireland almost to ruin.

Realising that his position and that of all the Geraldines was at stake, the Earl of Desmond immediately sent envoys to the kings of France and Scotland and to the Pope seeking help and military assistance, as he intended to become King of Ireland and drive out the English colonists. In A.D. 1345 after gathering all his forces and those of his allies, he marched to Kilkenny to seek the assistance of the other

Anglo-Irish lords, who were the descendants of the Anglo-Normans, in his quest to become King of Ireland, but all his pleas were rejected. Shortly afterwards Desmond was arrested in Dublin, as he was now outlawed and his earldom was considered forfeited. In June of that year Sir Ralf d'Ufford at the head of an English army marched into Munster. The Desmond Castle at Askeaton fell and, in November, Castleisland Castle in Kerry was taken. John Coterel, Eustace le Poer and William le Grant, who were in charge of the defences of Askeaton, were hanged, drawn and quartered. A general pardon was proclaimed in May 1346 to all those who had attended the Parliament in Kilkenny but the name of the Earl of Desmond was omitted. Having made a personal appeal to the King, both Desmond and Kildare were pardoned and both served with the English King at the siege of Calais.

From 1346, those that were staunch allies to the Crown fought numerous battles and skirmishes against the Irish and Anglo-Irish, but the arrival of the 'Black Death' in England hindered the recruitment of fresh soldiers for the Irish campaign. When the dreaded disease arrived in Ireland, the 'Black Death' caused the death of some 15,000 in Dublin in the space of four months. No figures are available for the rest of the country but it is reputed that three or four thousand died in the city of Limerick alone.

The Earl of Desmond, having returned home, died on the 25th January 1356 and was buried in Tralee without fulfilling his ambition to be King of Ireland. With the absence or extinction of the original grantees, the Desmond Fitzgeralds took over the vacant lordships like that of the Barony of Connello. In fact, the Desmond Fitzgerald held sway in all Munster, except for that part of Waterford held by de Poers. Backed by the junior branches of the family, like the Fitzgeralds of Kerry, of Glin, the Fitzgibbons of Kilmallock, the Barrys, Purcells, and the native Irish chieftains, they could not be brought down easily by any English king or army. In fact, these Anglo-Irish ruled the country as either Justiciars or Deputies from 1356 to 1361.

Maurice Fitzgerald was succeeded by Gerald, known in history as Gearoid Iarla, who was known as more of a poet than a leader. He ruled as Justiciar from 1367 to 1369. Although he was not inclined to warfare, he got involved with a dispute with Brian Ban O'Brien, the new King of Thomond, and a battle was fought outside Croom on 10th July 1370. Amidst great slaughter, Gerard was taken prisoner but was eventually ransomed. Brian captured the mainland part of Limerick city and placed Sida Og MacNamara in charge. After MacNamara was killed, Brian decided to retreat to his home territory with the spoils of Limerick and Desmond. When Brian died, he was succeeded by his son, Murrogh, who raided in all directions and made himself master of Clare, Munster, Connaught and most of Leinster by wiping out the large towns which were under English control.

Meanwhile Gerald Iarla spent most of his remaining days entertaining his guests with harpers, music, poetry and bardic recitals. He was now more Irish than the Irish themselves and his subsequent life and all the tales and legends are related in the following pages concerning his castles with their great halls of entertainment where every night was party night.

Lionel, second son of Edward III, was proclaimed King's Lieutenant for Ireland in 1361 and landed in Dublin in September with 1,500 men, under the command of the Earl of Stafford. He remained in Ireland for five years after a Proclamation was made that all Crown lands occupied by the Irish and all domains of non-residents were to be granted to English subjects. To attain this end he waged war in Desmond and against the clans of Leinster without much success. He left Ireland in November 1366.

Seeking the submission of the Anglo-Normans, who were now considered Anglo-Irish, King Richard II visited Kilkenny, which was the centre of the Irish government at that time. He received the submission and homage of the majority of the existing Irish princes or kings, which included the O'Neills, O'Connors, O'Briens, MacCarthys and others, but the Anglo-Irish, like the Geraldines from Munster, did not attend. This was considered as an insult to the Crown. After receiving the partial submission of Ireland, he sailed from Ireland on 15th May 1395.

A few years later, in 1398, Gerald, the Earl of Desmond, died in mysterious circumstances. It is reputed that he was poisoned. Within the year, his son and heir, Earl John, followed him to the grave having mysteriously drowned in the crossing of the Suir River. His daughter, Catherine, had already been banished from her home after being discovered in bed with her brother. She was banished and ended up in the care of the Earl of Ormond who raped her. In revenge she poisoned the Earl's beloved wife and then gradually took her place at the head of the household. John left a fourteen-year-old son called Thomas. He ruled as Earl of Desmond for ten years. Having married the daughter of one of his tenants, called Mac Cormac, he was forced to leave the country. James, the son of Gerald Iarla, who had been fostered by the O'Briens, seized the opportunity and declared himself Earl. Thomas found himself in England and, with the help of the Earl of Ormond, raised a small army and proceeded back to Desmond to reclaim his position as the rightful Earl of Desmond. However, the army of James was too strong and, in the ensuing battle, Thomas was taken prisoner. Having been released, Thomas returned to England and then travelled on to France to join his wife. He died in Paris in 1420 and the King of England attended his obsequies in the monastery of the Friars Preachers, due to the esteem he was afforded by the Crown. Thus ended the life a young man who was the pride and joy of all his subjects, who died in a foreign country due to his undying love for a beautiful peasant girl.

James ruled Desmond until 1462 with the assistance of the Knight of Kerry, the Knight of Glin, the White Knight and the O'Briens. The MacCarthys, O'Sullivans, O'Donoghues and the O'Donovans paid him tribute. To strengthen his army of horsemen and kerns he hired the gallowglasses, named MacSheehys, from Scotland. In fact, the whole province of Munster, with the alliance of the great Earls, was so strong that the English preferred to let them rule instead of invading and try to regain power.

When the Earl of Ormond arrived at Waterford in April 1420, he immediately summoned James of Desmond to be his ally. He made him Justice of the Peace for most of Munster and two years later made him Governor of the baronies. After assisting Ormond with over 5,000 soldiers in Leinster he was given the Constable-ship of the castle of Limerick. The Crown, by now, recognized him as a loyal subject, even though he continued to enlarge his earldom by driving out the English planters.

James was considered a great builder and restorer of castles, whether they were fortresses or residences. He rebuilt Askeaton and Newcastle where he added the noble hall that was called 'Halla Mor' in Irish. The income to pay for all this work was levied on all those living within his earldom. It was only with the Inquisition of 1583, when all of half a million acres of land in Munster were confiscated, that the true picture of the income to the Desmonds surfaced. He ruled most of the province like a palatine earl, or more like an Irish 'Ri', while being on the Council of Dublin amongst the Irish peers of State. He gave over the warden-ship of Carrigogunnel Castle and lands to his foster-brother Brian O'Brien. This parcel of land later became Pubblebrien with the Castle of Carrigogunnell as its capital. Married to a daughter of the Burkes (de Burgos) of Clanrichard, James had the Burkes as well as the O'Briens as allies, while the Earl of Kildare was his son-in-law; his position was unassailable. Desmond and the rest of Ireland, less a few exceptions, had lapsed into an aristocratic rule where the descendants of the old Anglo-Normans and the Irish chieftains were united in self-interest and preservation, each ruling his own territory or mini kingdom. There were some minor battles based on hereditary rights in the North but these were settled.

In 1449, Richard, Duke of York, landed at Howth with a small army. Many of the Irish chiefs came to pay homage and promised to assist him. Yet some of the Irish chiefs did not pay homage and Richard had to sue for terms in a battle at Trim where his army was overwhelmed. He departed Ireland in September 1450 without accomplishing very much. Ten years later, with the commencement of the War of the Roses – i.e., the conflict between the Houses of York and Lancaster for the English Throne – the Earl of Kildare continued as Deputy representing the Crown in Ireland. Which Crown is open to conjecture at this time, as England was in turmoil.

Richard, a defeated prince, landed in Ireland to seek help from the Irish and Anglo-Irish, and at the Parliament of Drogheda was confirmed as Viceroy of Ireland. In June 1460, he departed for England with many Irishmen in his

Ballygrennan Castle 1

Dysert Castle

train. With the English Crown almost within his grasp, he was killed at the battle of Sandal, near Wakefield, on 31st December that same year. However, his son, Edward, was crowned king in March 1461.

When James, the Earl of Desmond, died at Newcastle he was succeeded in 1462 by his son, Thomas, who was a loyal friend of Edward IV of England. In 1467, he was falsely accused of treason, and when he went to the enquiry in Drogheda, he was found guilty and beheaded on the 14th February 1468. In retaliation, his five sons, under James the eldest, gathered all the forces that they could muster in Munster and marched to Dublin, where they ravaged and then laid waste the Pale. James was later murdered at Rathkeale in 1487 on the instigation of his brother, Sir John Thomas, and was succeeded by his second brother, Maurice, 'Bacach' (lame). He put his brother John to death and ruled as the Earl of Desmond until 1520.

In 1491 a ship arrived in Cork carrying a young man who claimed that he was Richard, King Edward's son, who had escaped from the Tower of London. Many of the Irish declared for him, including Maurice, the Earl of Desmond, the White Knight, and the Knight of Glin. After a short stay in Munster he went to France, where King Maximilian recognised him as King of England. Some four years later he returned to Cork with eleven ships and, with the help of Desmond, besieged Waterford, which had declared for the Tudors. With the advance of Poynings with a large army from Dublin, he departed for Scotland. Later, King Henry VII announced a general pardon for all those who had assisted the imposter who became known as Warbeck. He was later executed at Tyburn in 1497.

Henry VIII came to power in April 1509. Being a youth of 18 years, he had no immediate interest in Ireland and the

Great Earl of Kildare continued to rule the country, with occasional marches with his army into Connaught, the Midlands and into Munster, where his ancestral homes were at Croom and Adare.

Following their actions in assisting Warbeck, the Munster Geraldines were stripped of power and Desmond was ruled by the Geraldines of Kildare, who were in favour with the House of York, until 1535. With the Geraldines of Desmond refusing to swear allegiance to the Crown they spent their time trying to motivate the other Anglo-Irish and Irish leaders in Munster to rise up in rebellion. When this was unsuccessful they sought help from the Continent. James, the eleventh Earl of Desmond, signed a treaty with Francis I of France offering mutual help and assistance against Henry of England, but this came to nothing.

In 1539, the thirteenth Earl of Desmond and O'Neill in the North came out in rebellion. This became known as the Geraldine League rebellion. When the promised help from France and Rome did not arrive the rebellion failed. Henry VIII of England demanded that all those who had taken part in the rebellion should renounce the Pope and his influence in Ireland. However, the Geraldines refused to comply. He also declared himself head of the church in Ireland about this time and ordered that a survey of all the monasteries be undertaken so that they could be dissolved, but the Geraldines refused to comply with this order as well.

In 1558, Garrett, the sixteenth Earl of Desmond, succeeded as heir, despite being the son by his father's second wife. It is reputed that James, his father, had at least four wives and many mistresses, following the example of Henry VIII. Garrett was a headstrong and impetuous young man and engaged himself in many petty rivalries, especially with his half-brother, Thomas Roe Fitzgerald, who had been disinherited by his father. He was about to engage the Earl of Ormond, his bitter enemy, in battle with over five thousand men only for the arrival of his first wife who happened to be a Butler. His second wife, Elinor, would later prove herself a strong character in aiding him when he was imprisoned in the Tower of London and later when he was on the run. She demonstrated her strong character by holding the house of Desmond together during those very troubled times.

Later, Garrett was released from the Tower and placed under house arrest in London during the period 1562-'64. During this short period he was allowed to visit the royal palace and even Elizabeth herself became one of his many admirers for his dashing and wild good looks, great sense of humour and knowledge, which even surpassed most of her own advisors. When he was released from house arrest in London, he was allowed to go to Dublin but still under house arrest. After a few months he gave his guards the slip and, without any escort, rode to his own domain in Limerick where he immediately called on all his allies for assistance. Soon he had a large army gathered and he marched into Ormond to gather rents and demand restitution of what was owing to him over the period of time that he was absent. After these adventures his conflict with the English Crown became a cause for religious freedom.

Having made his peace with Stukely, one of the adventurers who had been supplied with arms and an army by Henry VIII, he convinced him to go to Spain, France and to Rome to seek assistance against religious oppression, while he himself sought refuge in the wild and forested glens of Aherlow where he knew he would be safe. Meanwhile, the Earl of Ormond, who had been temporarily held in London, returned to Ireland. He immediately gathered an army and marched south into Limerick and Kerry where he was joined by the O'Sullivans and the Mac Carthys and they laid waste Limerick and Kerry. With this action began the decline of the rule of the Munster Geraldines.

In 1571, a group of new adventurers arrived in Cork. Their main objective was to enforce their rights, claiming that they were the descendants of the early Anglo-Norman invaders. Pursuing their claims for most of Munster and the Butler territory of Leinster, they presented false documentation. It is not known whether they were acting on their own initiative or if were being aided by Henry VIII. The immediate result was that Desmond rose up in rebellion once again sending envoys to Spain and Rome for assistance to fight for religious freedom.

Help came from Spain in the form of a large shipload of arms and ammunition and the struggle continued under the leadership of James Fitzmaurice, while the English forces who were led by Gilbert initiated a 'torched earth' policy in Desmond. In south Kerry, MacCarthy Mor joined Perott and they laid siege to Catlemaine Castle. This siege was abandoned after three weeks but the same force returned the following spring and the garrison surrendered, just before James Fitzmaurice and his force arrived. James finally surrendered at Aherlow and this short rebellion was over.

Queen Elizabeth released Fitzmaurice in 1573 but he was to remain under house arrest in Dublin. Eventually, he fled Dublin and returned to his Palatine territory and again took up the struggle against the Crown. Knowing that he could not hold on to his position on his own, he departed to France, Spain and Rome to seek assistance. Eventually, he was successful in getting about a thousand men and arms from Pope Gregory XIII. Stukely joined him and was put in charge of the expedition that sailed for Lisbon. Instead of sailing on to Ireland, Stukely joined the King of Portugal who was preparing to attack Morocco. Both Stukely and the young king were killed, as well as over half of the papal force.

On hearing of this disaster, Fitzmaurice departed from northern Spain with money, a papal delegate and some eighty men. Landing in Dingle in July 1579, he called for a Catholic revolt against the Crown and was soon joined by his brothers, Sir John and Sir James Fitzmaurice. Realising that help was necessary from Connaught, Sir James began his journey north but was killed by the Burkes of Castle Connell over a trade of horses. Within a short period of time the rebellion broke out in Connaught and parts of Leinster, but Fitzmaurice did not declare his hand – he knew that he was not strong enough to enter conflict with Sir William Pelham who was in charge of the Crown forces in Munster. Pelham, aware that Fitzmaurice could join the rebellion at any time, marched into Desmond and destroyed many of their castles and fortifications. He spared no one. In addition to the defenders, everyone found in the castles, including women and children, were put to the sword.

Thomas, the Earl of Ormond, returned from London and became Lord High Treasurer, President of Munster and Lieutenant of the Crown forces in Ireland. Known as 'An Thierna Dubh' or the Black Lord, he marched into Desmond and Kerry and headed for Dingle where he believed that Fitzmaurice was holding out. On his way south, he ordered that everyone encountered, including women, children and all animals, be killed and all houses and crops be burned. His atrocities were long remembered as the worst ever recorded in Desmond and Kerry.

Both Pelham and Ormond searched in vain for Fitzmaurice throughout Desmond and Kerry but he was always a step ahead of them. Remaining on the run he slept rough in the woods with a few servants and bodyguards. His brother John was in Wicklow aiding Lord Baltinglass in his revolt, while his wife sought shelter and protection from those she could trust.

On 13th September 1580 a fleet of ships, having avoided the English patrol, entered Smerwick Harbour in Kerry. They had been sent by the Pope and contained a force consisting mostly of Italians and Spanish with some Irish soldiers. They also brought with them a proclamation nominating the Earl of Desmond as papal lieutenant-general of Ireland. It is impossible to state why the Earl and his brother John did not join the landing force. In all probability they realised that if they moved their forces down to the end of the Dingle peninsula that they could be cut off by the English forces under Grey, who was already on the move.

Admiral Winter with the English ships at his disposal began to bombard the small fort at Dun-An-Oir which the newly arrived foreign force had reinforced, and soon Colonel Grey with the English force arrived by land. Amongst the English force was Walter Raleigh, who had already killed the infirm, women and children at the last English camp when they came searching for food. Seeing that their situation was untenable, the besieged offered to parley under a white flag. Terms were agreed whereby the foreigners, having been disarmed, would leave the country, but the Irish amongst them would be tried for sedition. When the surrender was agreed and all arms handed over, Grey ordered that everyone, including women and children, be hanged outside the fort as a warning to all. This was later considered one of the greatest disregards of the terms of warfare in Europe during the Middle Ages.

When word came through of the horrific events at Dun-An-Oir, the Earl of Desmond brought together what forces he could muster and carried out a type of guerrilla warfare on the English whereever he could. He did manage to inflict serious losses to the English forces, but cholera and dysentery caused the most deaths. In 1583, the Duke of Ormond took charge of the English forces in Munster and by the end of that summer the rebellion was crushed and the Earl of Desmond was on the run. When his camp was finally located he was beheaded and his head was taken to Cork. His body, however, was removed and buried in a secret location.

When the Desmond lands were confiscated by an Act of Parliament in Dublin, the adventurers moved in to claim what they could. However, those who had no involvement in the rebellion held most of the lands. They were allowed to hold on to their properties and only some two hundred thousand acres were in fact confiscated. Among those who received large parcels were Sir Walter Raleigh and Herbert. Meanwhile, Lady Elinor and her daughters, so used to the comforts of high living in their castles, were reduced to begging for food and shelter. When Queen Elizabeth heard about their plight she granted a pension of £200 per annum to Lady Elinor and two of her daughters received £50 per annum.

Most of the Desmond lands in Kerry and in west Limerick were entrusted to the Earl of Cloncarre, Mac Carthy Mor, who had not been involved in the Desmond Rebellion but had remained loyal to the Crown. Amongst the 'undertakers' who gained vast tracts of land in Limerick was a Thomas Brown, son of Sir Valentine Brown of Kerry.

In 1598, O'Neill rose in rebellion in the North and within a month or so most of the Desmond territory fell into Irish hands. Most of those displaced after the Desmond Rebellion regained their lands and castles. Sir Thomas Roe, Fitzgerald's son, claimed the title of Earl of Desmond. This was confirmed by O'Neill who was by now in possession of most of Ireland. In February 1599, Lord Mountjoy was sent to Ireland as Lord Deputy and Carew was made Lord President of Munster. Realising that Munster would prove the greatest threat, Mountjoy set about quelling the rebellion and within a few months Waterford, Tipperary and Limerick were regained. The 'Sugan Earl' was betrayed by the White Knight and sent to the Tower of London where he died some seven years later.

With news of the arrival of Spanish ships at both Castlehaven and Kinsale in County Cork, both O'Neill and O'Donnell gathered their armies and marched south to join the invasion force. Many of the Munster Irish leaders also rose out and headed for Kinsale when O'Neill passed through Limerick on his way south. Foraging for food on their way south both O'Neill and O'Donnell created many enemies amongst those Irish clans whose lands they laid waste. They were to pay dearly both in men, supplies and baggage on their way home after their defeat at Kinsale. But, nobody suffered more than O'Sullivan Bere on his epic march to Leitrim after the destruction of Dunboy Castle on the Beara peninsula.

Brouncker succeeded Carew, who was in ill health, as President of Munster in 1604. All the English 'undertakers' who had fled Ireland during 1601 were told to return to their lands. Many of them failed to return and those English landlords who held strong positions purchased their holdings or else claimed the lands as their own. Amongst these was Boyle of Cork, who acquired most of the lands of Sir Walter Raleigh for a paltry sum of £1,000.

The 'Sugan Earl'

James Fitzthomas Fitzmaurice was the son of an illegitimate son of the then Earl of Desmond. After the suppression of the Desmonds in 1583, James Fitzthomas petitioned Queen Elizabeth for the restoration of his possessions, i.e. the confiscated Earldom of the Desmonds. His petition was rejected, as it was the intention of the Crown to settle those lands with English planters.

After the uprising of the 'Sugan Earl' in 1601, when he was nominated the Earl of Desmond by Hugh O'Neill, he found himself at the head of some 8,000 clansmen and fought the English forces that were under the command of the Butlers, the Earl of Ormond, and Sir George Carew. He was defeated in the woods of Aherlow and fled to south Tipperary. Being pursued, he hid in one of the caves west of the now famous cave which attracts visitors from all over the world. Carew sought by every means to capture or kill the 'Sugan Earl' without success. However, he was betrayed by one of his kinsmen, Edmund Fitzgibbon, the White Knight, and was captured in his cave on the 20th May 1601.

In 1641 another rebellion broke out. This was partly religious and most of the Anglo-Irish in Munster joined. Limerick and Kerry joined in and both counties were soon in the hands of the rebels. Limerick Castle was besieged and eventually taken, after a wall was breached. Most of the other castles were taken and the English landowners fled to the safety of Cork and Dublin. A papal legate arrived in Kenmare Bay with arms and money for the uprising. However, the various parties, including the Roman Catholics, Royalists, the Protestant Loyalists and the small Puritan faction involved in the rebellion, began to argue amongst themselves. Soon the rebellion fell into disarray and the Parliamentarian army had success after success on the battlefield. The uprising continued until 1652 when Ludlow captured Ross Castle in Killarney, releasing all the defendants on the condition that they left the country.

When Charles I of England was beheaded and Cromwell gained power in England, few in Ireland knew what to expect. One of his first declarations was that the 'Irish problem' must be solved. He didn't mean the Irish alone, but the old Anglo-Irish and the English who were Roman Catholic or loyalists. After coming to Ireland he massacred all those who resisted him and his ultimate solution was to send everyone in Munster, Leinster and Ulster to Connaught. His campaign in Ireland was mostly financed by merchants, adventurers and bankers. On his return to England he devised a plan to repay his debts by offering his backers large tracts of land in Ireland. This was to become known as the Cromwellian Settlement.

When he departed to England he left his son-in-law, Ireton, to continue his work. Having been reinforced by more troops from England, Ireton captured Kilmallock and Castleconnell and waited for his opportunity of capturing Limerick. This was to happen in April 1651. A formal summons to surrender was rejected. After various attempts to assault the castle, Ireton decided on a blockade and surrounded the city which, incidentally, had over a year's supply of food within its walls. Disease and plague affected both those inside the walls and in the English camp. With winter approaching and his army dwindling, Ireton decided to make one last assault with the large cannons which were brought ashore from the English warships. A breach was made in the walls and the English entered. A surrender was negotiated whereby the inhabitants were allowed to leave, the soldiers were to lay down their arms, the officers could retain their swords and some twenty-four leaders were condemned to death. After the fall and Ireton's death from the plague, Sir Hardress Waller, who held substantial territory around Limerick, was made Governor of Limerick.

After the ignominious defeat at the Boyne, King James, who had not participated in the battle, fled south to Kinsale to take ship to France with his entourage and most of his French officers. The defeated Irish army marched westward and crossed the Shannon. Athlone and Limerick were still in Irish control. William, meanwhile, also moved south to the Shannon, with Limerick as his prime objective as he considered the city as the centre of Irish rebellion. Both armies were about the same size with twenty thousand men but William had light artillery. His main siege guns were being brought from Cashel protected by two troops of dragoons. William was of the opinion that as soon as he arrived outside the walls of Limerick with his large cannons that the Irish would surrender. On 9th August, the main English force advanced against the city. Two field pieces of artillery were brought up and began to fire on the Irish positions and more were brought to bear on walls and the interior. The following morning a deserter from the English camp brought the news that the heavy guns and ammunition were expected from Cashel. Sarsfield gathered his elite force of horsemen together and slipped out of Limerick during the night and encountered the wagon train the following day. Waiting for nightfall he launched a surprise attack killing most of the dragoons and then destroyed the large cannons and ammunition. He then returned to Limerick. Meanwhile, Castleconnell Castle was surrendered without a fight.

William ordered that more heavy guns be brought from Waterford and, while awaiting their arrival, he began to fortify his positions around the city and made a few attempts to gain entry. Then, on 27th August, the main assault was made but was driven back with a great loss of life on both sides. Finally, seeing that he could not take the city without a greater loss of life, the river being in flood and with winter approaching, he lifted the siege.

In May of the following year (1691) the English army came together at Mullingar under Ginkle while King James sent three French officers and a small number of soldiers to Limerick as a token of assistance. After taking Athlone again, Ginkle marched to Limerick where he found the city refortified with the Irish cavalry on the Clare side and the Irish infantry outside and within the walls. On 27th August both Carrigogunnel and Castleconnell surrendered and were blown up with gunpowder.

On 8th September all the English cannons were brought to bear on the city defences and this bombardment was continued until the 12th, but no major breach was made. When the Irish cavalry were forced to leave, William issued a proclamation detailing a surrender and the terms. There was no reply. When a breach was finally made and the English and Continental troops from the Low Countries and Denmark plus the German auxiliaries advanced in numbers, no quarter was given on either side. The slaughter continued for hours on end until about a thousand men on both sides were killed. On 27th September the Irish and the English commenced negotiations for peace and on 3rd October the infamous Treaty of Limerick was signed by both parties. This Treaty, even though ratified by William and Mary, was violated by the English House of Commons after three thousand of the Irish soldiers returned home to Connaught and the majority of the remaining fourteen thousand left for service in France and on the Continent.

Thus came to an end one of the bloodiest periods of Munster history, which saw the demise of the Irish Clans, the Anglo-Irish and those who had fought for religious freedom. Much more hardship and persecution was to come.

In the following pages are the details of the castles and tower-houses of Limerick and much more of the history of Limerick city and county.

The Knights Templar

No history of Limerick County or that of Ireland could be complete without reference to the Knights Templar and the Knights Hospitaller. They came to Ireland with the Norman knights dressed in their full armour with a red cross portrayed on their slip-over gown of white colour.

It is not known why they came in such numbers. Maybe many of them were somehow related to the Norman knights who had taken part in the Crusades. The Knights were a type of warrior monk on horseback whose original aim was to protect Christians travelling to the Holy Land following the announcement from Pope Urban II that a Crusade against the 'infidels' who held the Holy Places would be launched in 1096. The Templars were not normal monks but took the monastic vows of poverty, chastity and obedience. Even though the Templars had taken a vow of poverty they accumulated much wealth.

Jerusalem and other principalities in the Middle East were subdued. After some time the Knights Templars became the guardians of the Holy Places, especially in Jerusalem for the Pope. From their possession of the Holy Places in Jerusalem it is reputed that they discovered and retrieved the Holy Grail and the Ark of the Covenant which contained the two slabs of stone on which the Ten Commandments were impressed by the hand of God.

Their Order grew from strength to strength and soon they had established themselves along the route to the Holy Land and also in Cyprus where they built churches and stone fortifications which were used by pilgrims. By the time they had established themselves in Italy, France, England, etc.

they had accrued much wealth, so much so that they became almost independent of Rome and of the European monarchs. In fact, they became the founders of the banking system and money lending profession whereby they gained more and more wealth. The Templars took part in all the Crusades from c. 1096 to 1270 CE. How they and their horses in armour survived the extreme heat of the Middle East in summer must lead one to believe that they were extremely fit and strong as they wielded their heavy swords going into battle.

We do not know if they came to Ireland with the first contingent of Norman knights or accompanied King John when he landed near Wexford. Yet, by 1270, they had established themselves in Munster where they built their castles and churches, including Askeaton and others in counties Limerick, Cork, Kerry and Waterford. In Limerick County alone they had over twenty establishments. Even though the Templar stone castles and churches were based on early Norman architecture, they were very different and unique. Their castles were either square or round at the base rising into a hexagonal or octagonal apex or visa versa. Why? Maybe it was to indicate to foreign travellers that they were approaching a refuge in the control of the Templars!

When we examine the castles of the Military Orders of the Knights Templars and the Knights Hospitallers in Limerick and elsewhere in Munster, we find some unusual type of building – hexagonal, octagonal or square outside and the reverse inside – mostly round. Some exteriors changed into round building outside after a few metres. Mostly they had cellars and basements and some had tunnels running underground to another nearby building or church, regardless of the distance, like in the ancient city of Acre which was their main establishment in the Middle East. Many caverns or underground passageways were to be found under their castles, but to our knowledge no archaeological survey has been carried out on these in Ireland up to the present day. They only built walls around their churches, commandaries, and preceptories in lands where there was no strong governing power and where they were prone to be attacked by enemy forces.

Amongst the early Anglo-Normans to come to Ireland during the thirteenth and fourteenth centuries who were related to the Knights Templars were de Roche, Fitzstephens, De Lacys, Hamo, d'Arcy, and de Burgos.

The first mention of the Templars and Hospitallers in the royal administration records for Ireland was in 1220. They had come over to take up the role of administrators for Henry III, as they were the only ones he could trust. They were allocated land and founded a number of commandaries. The Viceroy of Ireland was instructed to deposit all royal dues into the care of the Templars and Hospitallers who would send it to England. This was similar to the duties that they carried out in England for King Henry. Care of cash or acting as negotiators or ambassadors for the kings of Europe were normal duties for the Templars. In England, Brother Geoffrey of the Templars was one of the main advisors to King Henry. While the Templars were engaged in financial matters for the King, the Knights Hospitallers were administrators and were given military command against Irish attacks. The Templars refrained from any military action against other Christians. On the other hand the Hospitallers of St. John joined in any action ordered by the King.

It was not unusual to find mills near the establishments of the Knights Templars or Hospitallers. They were a source of income. In addition to grinding wheat and barley from the Templars lands they were also rented out and this gave them an additional source of revenue. In Limerick County we find a number of mills which were mostly owned and operated by the Templars. These have been mentioned in the context of particular castles or establishments.

The Templars and the Knights of St. John were not subject to the local bishops in County Limerick and elsewhere. They were subject only to the Pope and the King. This gave rise to a certain amount of envy and mistrust.

When the Order of the Temple was banned by Philip IV of France and was suppressed by Pope Clement V in 1312 this gave rise to persecution, including burning at the stake in most of the European countries, including Ireland. In County Limerick, at the instigation of the bishops, there were mock trials where the Templars were accused of blasphemy, heresy, sodomy and stealing from the poor. There are stories that some knights were burned at the stake by the common people while their castles and lands fell into the hands of the bishops. This, however, would be at varience with what happened in England where no torture was used and must therefore be doubted.

Nothing over the recent centuries has caught the imagination more than the myths or legends associated with the Knights Templar. They were supposed to be the protectors of the Holy Grail and the Ark of the Covenant, which were reputed to have been moved around Western Europe in times of trouble and were hidden in the secret chambers of their castles or churches. The myths or legends of the Templars are in complete contradiction with the more ancient legend that the prophet Josephus fled from Egypt with the Ark of the Covenant and journeyed to the western Mediterranean and then disappeared from the pages of history. However, here in Ireland there are legends that he actually arrived on the south coast with his followers, as well as the Ark of the Covenant. Maybe this influence of the Hebrews might explain why the ancient Irish language had so many Hebrew words.

For those people interested, the following is an approximate list of locations where the Knights Templar and Knights Hospitallers or Knights of St. John of Jerusalem had established themselves during the thirteenth century in County Limerick:

Adare
Ainy – a Preceptory
Askeaton – Commandery founded in 1298
Ballingarry
Ballycahane
Ballynoe
Bruff – at Templebodean (1284)
Bruree – Castle and Temple Colman
Carrig-a-Quincy – Kilkeedy Parish – Castle
Carrickketal
Carrigogunnel
Castle Matrix
Castlemeine
Castle Rag
Dysert
Glenogra
Hospital
Kileedy – at nearby Trand
Kildimo – Small Templar Church built in 1290 on O'Donovan's land
Kilquane Parish – church north of Mount Russell
Limerick – A house in Quay Lane
Listeely – Kildromin Church
Morgans – Templemuireguiedan

Mungret – Temple Mungret
Newcastle – a commandery
Rathurd
Shanid – possibly
Woodstock

Division of Land

Up to the time of the Anglo-Normans the division of land in Ireland was according to the amount of territory that each Clan or family chieftain held. In fact, according to the best available sources, there were about 186 divisions of land. Some were extensive and held by powerful chieftains, while others were under the control of minor clan leaders who paid homage to the local powerful Clan leader in cattle, crops, women and military duty when required. This division was adopted by the ecclesiastical authorities and even up to today still exists as dioceses. The division of land into provinces, counties, baronies, parishes and townlands was implemented by the Anglo-Normans. In the time of Queen Elizabeth the province of Munster was divided into five English shires – Tipperary, Limerick, Waterford, Kerry, and Cork, with Desmond, Ormond and Thomond. The church was responsible for the parochial division. With the submission of the Irish chieftains their territories were called baronies. The baronies of Limerick County were Coonagh, Owneybeg, Clanwilliam, Small County, Coshlea, Coshma, Pubblebrien, The Liberties of Limerick City, Kenry and Connello. This last was divided into Upper and Lower Connello and also split into 'divisions' such as Shanid.

Castles and Fortified Houses (alphabetical)

Abington / Woney / Butler's Castle
Parish: Abington
Townland: Abington or Farnane
Barony: Oneybeg
OS Sheet 65 somewhere around ref 720 545

In the district of Woney the castle commanded an important route between Clanwilliam on one side and Ormond on the other. The castle was built by the Butlers and partly demolished by the Earl of Ormond, Lord Justice of Ireland, in 1452 when it was in the possession of Conor O'Mulryan.

The O'Mulryans, however, held on to their possessions in this area until 1600 when their castles were destroyed and the whole clan was put to the sword.

The abbey of Woney deserves to be mentioned here. It was founded by the Fitzwalters, lords of Carrick, in 1205 for the Cistercian order. It was furnished from the abbey at Savigniac in France. The founder was buried within its walls in 1206, so too was the Chief of the Butlers in 1299. In 1548 the O'Carrolls marched from Nenagh and, having taken possession of most of that territory, ordered the Ormonds (Butlers) to leave that part of the country.

As the result of an inquisition held in Rathkeale on 23rd August 1592, a Peter Walshe was dispossessed of his lands, which included his castle at Woney and the monastery called Woney. In 1647 part of Lord Inchiquin's forces stormed the castle and burned the abbey.

The abbey and lands were granted to the Stepney family. Sometime later, they demolished the abbey and built Abington house with the materials. Today, hardly anything remains of the famous house, abbey or castle.

See also Castle Comfort and Rath Castle.

Adare Castle

Adare: Ath-Dara – the ford of the Oak
Barony: Coshma
OS Sheet 65 ref 470 467
Situated on the banks of the Mague River nine miles from Limerick.
Castle situated just north of Adare, close to the N21.

The castle ruins are found on the east bank of the Mague River near the old bridge. It appears that the castle was first built on the site of an ancient fort or rath. This original fortification was reputedly built by the O'Donovans c. 1202, but the second Earl of Kildare rebuilt the stone castle in 1326.

It was enlarged and fortified many times. One of the earliest descriptions of the castle dates from c. 1331 and mentioned that 'there was a castle in which there was a large hall, a thatched chapel, a slated kitchen, a thatched chamber and a tower covered with planks'. In 1657 the castle was dismantled by the orders of Cromwell. It is said that the south-eastern corner by the river was bombarded by cannon fire. The castle has been in ruins ever since.

The ruins consist of a group of buildings. The castle had an outer and inner ward or bawn and was a good example of a mediaeval fortress with its crenellated cur-

PLAN OF ADARE CASTLE

Legend:
- 1200
- 1400
- LATE MEDIEVAL

KEEP

OUTER YARD

HALL

HALL

tain wall. Here there are two great halls in addition to a kitchen, a bakery and stables. The oldest of the halls had early thirteenth century windows, round-headed, and with sandstone mouldings. Within the inner ward was a strong square castle. Also within the walls were a portcullis, stables, kitchen and a dungeon. Also, the castle had a drawbridge. The river and a moat formed the outer defences. Work has taken place in recent centuries to preserve the ancient ruin.

The castle was originally built to protect the fords across the river. Adare was the ancient home of the Hy-Cairbre. Cathal, a chief of the Hy-Cairbre, married a daughter of Amlaf, King of the Norsemen in Munster. Their son, Donovan, lived at Bruree. He was killed by Brien Boru of the Dalcassian. Another clan called the O'Quins of Inchiquin, in Clare, were driven out of their homeland and settled in Limerick, Kilmallock and Adare. After the death of Donovan, his clan lost its importance and was later dispossessed of their lands by the Anglo-Normans. They migrated south into Kerry and West Cork, especially around Carbery.

Adare is mentioned in a grant made to one Jeffrey de Morreis by Henry III in 1226 to hold a fair. Mention again in 1310 in a grant issued by Edward II for the levy of tolls and tariffs for the building of a wall around the town. In 1576 the town was levelled to the ground by the Irish and, later that century, by Torlough O'Brien, but the town was regained. The castle was then in the hands of the Geraldines. Thomas, the eighth Earl and Lord Deputy died in the castle in 1477.

Gerald, the ninth Earl of Kildare, supported Perkin Warbeck's claim to the throne of England, was accused of treason and all his possessions were forfeited to the crown. He was, however, restored to his estate by Henry, Prince of

Wales, who made him deputy-governor of Ireland. In 1519 this Gerald was made Lord Deputy and given the task of capturing his nephew, the Earl of Desmond, then in rebellion and holed up in the Castle of Askeaton. He failed in this, which together with other charges led to his imprisonment in the Tower of London, where he died. Before leaving for London he had handed over his duties to his son, Thomas Fitzgerald, known as 'Silken Thomas', who immediately led a revolt against the Crown but this failed miserably and he, himself and five of his uncles were put to death in the Tower of London.

In 1527, the then Earl of Desmond took possession of Adare and made his submission to the king. Adare had been forfeited to the Crown, yet Desmond was allowed to remain in possession and became Lord Treasurer of Ireland. During the Elizabethan wars the English often attacked Adare Castle, and in the summer of 1578 it was taken after a siege of eleven days. The following year Carew commanded a strong garrison there. He was himself besieged by Irish forces under Sir John Desmond but this attack was repulsed. In 1581 the Irish forces finally captured the castle and slaughtered the garrison. English forces under Colonel Zouch had arrived from Cork too late to raise the siege but attacked the confederate forces of the Earl who were in possession of the castle and inflicted a severe defeat on them in the process.

On the death of Gerald in 1583, the Earls of Kildare regained possession of Adare Castle and lands until 1683. O'Neill of Tyrone, when he was in revolt, came to Adare and conferred the title of Earl of Desmond on James Fitzgerald who became known as the 'Sugan Earl'. A number of battles were fought in the vicinity of Adare between the English forces and those of Desmond but nothing decisive. The castle was abandoned by Sir George Carew sometime later but was again reoccupied by the English, who had to sustain a long siege without food or water. In 1600 the town was burned to the ground by English forces under the command of Maurice Stack. It was taken over again by the Irish during the Rebellion of 1641 but was recaptured by the forces of the Earl of Castlehaven. In 1657 the castle was dismantled on the orders of Oliver Cromwell. The great house later known as Adare Castle was built in the 1830s.

Old Legend
Some have tried to connect the origins of the name of Adare with Ath-Tarbh, the Ford of the Bull. In earlier times, there was legend of a fire-eating bull. This monster had his base at Carrig-o-Gunnell and ravaged all the countryside around. When St. Patrick came to the area he exorcised the beast and drove it out of its territory.

St. Patrick is said to have followed the evil bull and in its attempt to escape across the Maigue River it drowned, as no evil thing was able to cross running water.

Amigan (Amogan) Castle
Parish: Croagh: Cruach – a round hill
Townland: Amogan More
Barony: Lower Connello East
OS Sheet 64 ref 397 413
The ruins of this castle were supposed to be located about 4 kilometres east of Rathkeale town.

This was a tower house where James I is reputed to have slept for a night after his defeat at the Boyne, although Lewis casts doubts on the veracity of this tale, as most accounts have him going directly to Kinsale, County Cork, where he embarked for France.

Ardpatrick Castle
Parish: Ballingaddy: Baile an Ghadaidhe – town of the thief
Townland: Ballingaddy
Barony: Coshma / Coshlea
OS Sheet 73 ref 642 212

Very little is known about this castle or where it was located. The map reference above is the probable area, close to the ancient church, holy well and round tower.

The only mention of the castle is by Smith in his *Miscellaneous Limerick Papers*, which states that 'in 1198, the English built the Castle of Ard Patrick in Munster'.

Askeaton Castle
Parish: Askeaton: Eas Cead Tine – Waterfall of a Hundred Fires
Eas Geitine – Waterfall of the Geitine – ancient tribe
Barony: Lower Connello east
OS Sheet 64 ref 342 503

Askeaton Castle was built c. 1199, according to *the Annals of Inishfallen*. This seems to have been a wooden structure with a rampart and moat. It was first occupied by an Anglo-Norman knight by the name of Hamo de Valoignes from Suffolk in England. From 1197 to 1199 he was the chief Justiciary for Ireland.

Shortly afterwards William de Burgo was in occupation and built a castle of stone on the same site, which is a small island mainly of limestone encircled by two branches of the river Deel. A sort of motte was constructed around part of the island with a defensive wall.

The ruins that are to be seen today date from the sixteenth century. A high wall enclosed the whole area. Inside were the Constables Tower of three storeys, another tower which has vanished, and the Desmond Tower house which was of five storeys.

All that remains of the tower house is the south wall section, which reveals the remains of three large vaulted rooms on the ground floor. There is no indication that the first floor room was vaulted but it had a massive fireplace and a very large window. There are some fine windows seats in embrasures. Some of the traceried windows were among the most elaborate in any Irish castle.

West of the tower house are the ruins of the banqueting hall ('An Teach Midhchuarta') which was built over the arches of an earlier hall later converted into 'the Desmond Wine Cellars'. The hall has some beautiful carved windows and a blind arcade in the south wall. In the outer bawn was the Hall Mor or banqueting hall, which probably had a thatched roof. This was built by James, the seventh Earl of Desmond c. 1440. It measured approximately 24 metres by 9.5 metres and was one of the finest examples of medieval architecture in Ireland. There were also remains of a court or dwelling house connected with the main tower castle, and some 25 metres away were the remains of another

Askeaton Castle

tower. All the castle towers and banqueting halls were supposed to have been enclosed by a great wall but now nothing remains of this structure.

Donal Mor O'Brien, King of Thomond, arranged the marriage between his daughter and William de Burgo thus reinforcing his position as king. The stone castle was refortified around this time within the moat and rampart. This use of the ancient moat and rampart was copied at Glin and Carrigogunnell. The nearby Templar church with its unusual stone tower was founded c. 1270. According to the Four Masters this was replaced by an Abbey built by the Earl of Desmond in 1420 for the Franciscans where he erected a tomb for himself and his family.

Sometime later, Hugo de Neville was in occupation of the castle for a number of years. In 1287 the castle was granted to Thomas de Clare who was married to Juliana, daughter of Maurice Fitzgerald, the third Baron of Offaly. King Edward II granted Askeaton Castle to Robert de Welle in 1308 but it was back in the hands of Richard de Clare in 1315. De Clare was killed in the battle of Dysart in 1318. His wife, Lady de Clare fled to England, but not before having Bunratty Castle set on fire. She still, however, retained possession of Askeaton Castle. In that same year the Templar church at Askeaton was burgled by a Roger Cromple and some associates searching for valuables. Later he was apprehended but fled the country before being sentenced.

In 1322 Edward II granted the castle to Lady de Clare's son and daughter. By 1348 Maurice Fitzgerald was in possession of the massive fortress which had replaced the original castle, and from this year onwards it became the main home of the Munster Geraldines. Maurice had earlier married a daughter of Murrough O'Brien, King of Munster, called Lafracoth. Their third son, also called Maurice,

Askeaton Castle

Ballingarry Castle

became the founder of the Fitzgerald line and was appointed Lord Lieutenant of Ireland in 1355. It is reputed that the castle was rebuilt under his instructions.

In 1580 on 3th April, the Duke of Ormond laid siege to the castle. The garrison deserted and most of the castle was destroyed by cannon, except the main tower. Having left four companies at Askeaton, the Lord Justice returned to Limerick on 5th April. After a short rest he made his way down the river to Adare while Captain Case followed with the troops by land. According to the *Four Masters*, every living person encountered was killed while all the cattle and sheep were driven back to Limerick.

Shortly afterwards Pope Gregory, the thirteenth, granted to all Irishmen who would fight against Elizabeth, the same plenary pardon and remission of all their sins as those who had joined the Crusades against the Turks.

The Knights Templars had also settled at Askeaton where they established a Commandery in 1298. Almost nothing remains except for an unusual tower which existed near the ancient parish church. The lower part of the tower is square but from about six feet high it changes into an octagonal structure. It has loop holes on three sides while on the fourth side was a low circular arched doorway which connected the tower to the old church which was also reputed to belong to the Templars. The church is said to have been originally from even earlier times. The Templars were accustomed to getting control of food supplies so they had a mill built which they operated with local help.

At Askeaton the tenth Earl of Desmond signed a treaty with the French king, Francis I. It was stipulated that Desmond would make war on Henry VIII and that the French would make a landing in Ireland. This was ratified in St-Germain-en-Laye in 1524. This agreement came to nothing.

During the Geraldine rebellion some forty-five years later, the Desmond forces were defeated at Manister on 3rd October 1579 by Malby, who was the English Governor of Connaught. After the battle, Gerald, the fifteenth Earl of Desmond, sought refuge in his castle at Askeaton. Unable to take the castle due to lack of cannon, Malby torched the town and friary. Early in April of the following year Commander Pedlam and the English forces with their cannons took possession of the castle after a short siege of two days. In 1599, it was again besieged for over 247 days by the 'Sugan Earl' of Desmond, but he was unable to gain possession from the English forces within. In 1642 when the Irish forces took possession of Limerick Castle they also acquired a number of cannons. Now they had the means to attack the castles where the English had taken refuge. Amongst the cannons was a piece of some 404 kilo, which could shoot a ball of 14.5 kilo. This was probably the biggest cannon in Ireland at that time and had been mounted on Limerick Castle walls for defensive purposes. The only problem was that it lacked a carriage. Improvising, a huge tree was hollowed out and the gun was placed inside. This was pulled by twenty-five yoke of oxen over bogs, marshes, streams and rough terrain. With the arrival of this monstrosity near their walls, castle after castle surrendered. Cappagh opened its gates, Castle Matrix was yielded up, Askeaton surrendered and Kilfinny hung out a white flag after receiving four direct hits from the great cannon on 29th July 1642.

In 1652 Askeaton fell to the Cromwellian forces, who used gunpowder to blow up parts of the defences.

It is related that, during one of the minor encounters between the Earl of Desmond and the Earl of Ormond, the Earl of Desmond found himself besieged in his castle stronghold. His harper opened one of the gates on the condition

Tower at Askeaton Castle

that he should be raised higher than his master. When the harper asked for his reward he was immediately hung from the highest battlement. Desmond, meanwhile, succeeded in escaping from the castle carrying his wife, the countess, on his horse. However, she was seriously wounded by an arrow and when Desmond rode through the south gate of Mainistir an gCailleach Dubh, thinking that she had passed away she was hastily buried under the altar of the chapel. According to legend, the countess had been only unconscious and had been buried alive. Her spirit is said to haunt the location ever since.

Athlacca Castle
Parish: Athlacca
Townland: Unknown
Barony: Coshma
OS Sheet 65 in the area of ref 558 343

This was a de Lacey family castle which was in ruins by 1650. They also had a castle at Tullerboy, 2 kilometres to the north.
   See also Rathcannon which is 2 kilometres to the east.

Aughanish Castle
Parish: Aughinish / Each-Inis – horse island (Also referred to as 'Fanadh Mor')
Townland: Aghanish
Barony: Lower Connello
OS Sheet 64 ref 285 532

The castle was situated on an island in the Shannon now occupied by a major shipping terminal. This castle has almost completely disappeared from the landscape. It was attacked by the Irish Confederate forces during the rebellion of the 1640s and also attacked during Elizabeth's reign.

The earliest available reference to this castle is dated 1584. It was occupied at that time by a Tadhg O'Donoghue or Tadhg O'Duffie. In 1604 it was in the possession of R. Lister subject to the life interest of his mother Margaret Burke. In 1613 it was in the hands of Sir J.J. Jepson as part of his estate around Old Abbey. It changed hands again in 1616 after the Desmond Rebellion and became the property of the Berkeleys, who were constables of Askeaton Castle. By 1642 it was in the possession of George Courtney and in that year it was besieged by the Irish Confederates. Nicholas Mead, who was in charge of the defence, was forced to surrender. Up to the time of the Cromwellian confiscations it was in the hands of a family by the name of Dundon but was then given to a Cromwellian soldier by the name of Colonel Courtney. We do not know if he was a relation to the original Courtneys.

It is interesting to note that in the Civil Survey of 1840 not a single ruin of either church or castle was to be seen.

Baggotstown Castle
Parish: Knockainy: Cnoc Áine – hill of Áine
Townland: Baggotstown
Barony: Small County
OS Sheet 65 ref 660 350
This castle was situated about 2 kilometres southwest of Knockainy Castle.

The castle was in a ruinous condition in 1840. The east and the south walls only were standing. Measuring about 10 × 7.5 metres it had an addition of a square tower at its northeast corner. A stone arch remained of this tower on the ground floor. The castle was about 20 metres in height and had five storeys. The walls were 2 metres thick and some oak beams still remained. Described as a double structure with arched naval stairs, an extension was added sometime during the Tudor period. This had cross-barred mullioned windows and a bartizan at an angle. There were five chimneys on the gables with open ribbed crowns, which indicate that they were from the later period. The whole structure formed two sides of a square. O'Donovan came to the conclusion that the castle was defended by an outer wall but this has long since disappeared into the marshy ground.

The castle was built by the Baggot family c. A.D. 1619. A John Baggot attended the General Assembly of the Confederates in Kilkenny in January 1647. He also took part in signing the Articles of Limerick with Ireton on 27th October 1641. His son, Maurice, was exempt from the general pardon granted at the surrender of Limerick and all the Baggot lands and castle were forfeited.

Ballinard (Ballynard) Castle
Parish: Ballinard / Baile an Aird – town on the height
Townland: Ballinard
Barony: Small County
OS sheet 65 ref 687 415
Situated close to Herbertstown and 5 kilometres east of Lough Gur.

The ancient church of this parish was located on top of a hill about half a mile from Herbertstown. About two hundred metres or so further south was the site of the castle. Nothing remained in O'Donovan's time, but Fitzgerald refers to the low ruins of a castle on this site. Lewis ascribes its building to the fifteenth century. The castle was the residence of the Fitzgeralds of Ballinard. The last of this family was William Fitzgerald who was the High Sheriff of the County of Limerick in 1778 and Mayor of Limerick in 1786.

Ballingarry Castle
Parish: Ballingarry
Townland: Knightstreet
Barony: Upper Connello
OS sheet 65 ref 413 361

Ballingarry Castle, according to tradition, was built by the Knights Templar. It is said that the name of the townland and a street in the village called Knight Street derive from the Templars. After the suppression of the Order the castle was taken over by the Desmonds until they forfeited all their lands after their rebellion.

The De Lacys gained possession of Ballingarry at the end of the thirteenth century. Two other branches of that family took control of the areas of Bruff and Bruree and became the underlords of the Desmonds and supported them in their various uprisings against the Crown. They lost everything in the Cromwellian confiscations. The castle was the most southerly in the Barony of Connello in the possession of the Desmonds. It was built to protect an important pass in the chain of hills that stretched from Croom to Newcastle West which was the main means of communication between northern and southern Connello.

The ancient castle still stood there in 1896 and was in good condition. The castle was repaired and modernised early in the nineteenth century. This was a tower house measuring about 11.4 metres by 8 metres. On the third floor there was a substantial hall with a large window embrasure, which probably contained an altar. The other embrasures have seating and two-lighted windows. A spiral stairway descends to the entrance and the cellar or basement. The stair to the battlement is added out over the angle of the end wall and a wing containing a chamber and latrine. On the north side there was a square tower with its North West side being a continuation of the wall of the castle. This tower was about 20 metres in height and has a number of small square windows. The walls of the castle itself were just less than 4 feet thick. The castle contains three storeys, with the second storey having a plastered arch. The third floor contained a chimney that was fitted on the orders of a Mr. Gibbons who used the castle as a dwelling house. All of the above indicate that Ballingarry was built in the time of Elizabeth or later and the castle, as it survived into modern times, could not have been built by the Knights Templar. There could of course have been a previous Templar structure on the site, as it is recorded that a preceptory of the Knights Templar was founded here in 1172 which would make it probably the earliest in Limerick County.

This castle was destroyed along with Bruree Castle on the orders of Ginkle in 1691 during the siege of Limerick. In 1602, after the Fall of Dunboy Castle and the forced march of O'Sullivan Bere to Leitrim, Garret Stack still held on to the castle at Ballingarry but when Wilmot appeared with a large army the garrison surrendered.

Ballingarry Castle

Also in Ballingarry was Parson's Castle, so called because in the eighteenth century it was the residence of the rector. Earlier history unknown.

Also, 'the turret', which was a round tower building erected by a branch of the DeLacey family.

Ballyallinan Castle
Parish: Rathkeale / Rath Gaela
Townland: Ballyallinan
Barony: Connello Lower
OS Sheet 64 ref 347 377
Situated about 4.5 kilometres south of Rathkeale town.

Ballyallinan Castle measured about 11 metres by 5 metres. The walls were over 16 metres high and 2 metres thick. The castle had five floors with the first above the ground being arched.

It is said that it originally belonged to the O'Hallinans and was then taken over by the MacSheehys. It probably became a Desmond castle sometime later. Eddy II De Lacy married Ellen, daughter of Rory Mac Sheehy of Ballyallinan Castle. The Mac Sheehys were notable gallowglasses in the service of the Earls of Desmond. They wore shirts of mail, skullcaps of steel, and were armed with a dagger and a six-foot battle-axe. The Mac Sheehys suffered great losses at the battle of Monaister, outside of Croom, when Sir Nicholas Malby defeated the Desmond Geraldines.

In 1600 this castle was taken from Rory Mac Sheehy by Dermot O'Connor who planned to deliver the 'Sugan Earl' into the hands of the English, but he was besieged there and his own followers forced him to surrender. Later that year

(1600), Carew captured James Fitzgerald, the 'Sugan Earl' together with two Sheehy brothers and took possession of Ballyallinan Castle.

Ballybricken Castle / Old Court Castle
Parish: Cahirelly / Ballybricken
Townland: Ballybricken South
Barony: Clanwilliam
OS Sheet 65 ref 654 459

This castle was situated on a level field in the townland of Ballybricken South and measured about 5 × 5 metres inside. The height was 16 metres and the walls were 2.5 metres thick. It had four storeys and the one over the ground floor had an arch.

Ballycahane Castle
Parish: Ballycahan: Baile Ui Chatathain – town of O'Cahan
Townland: Ballyculhane Upper
Barony: Small County and Pubblebrien
OS Sheet 65 ref 547 446

This castle was situated about 7.5 kilometres northeast of Croom, and was built in 1496 by the O'Grady Family. A couple of kilometres to the southwest near Tory hill are the remains of a Templar church. Lewis mentions the many 'strange traditions' associated with the nearby Lough Nagirra without going into any details.

Donncadh O'Brien, who took over the territory and castle,

divided most of his lands amongst his ten sons. His eleventh son, Dermot, being without offspring, did not come into the equation. Ballycahane, as well as other parcels of land, went to his son, Brian, and was described as being north of the stream which flowed through the area. Two small castles appear in the early maps not far from each other. One of the sons, called Mahon, who had acquired Killonaghan, as well as other parcels of land from his father, was a friend of John Fitzgerald, Earl of Desmond, who had married an O'Brien, called Maire. He succeeded his father and took over Castle-gunnel Castle. He became known as 'Mago'.

Ballyclogh (Knocknagaul) Castle 1
Parish: Knocknagaul / Cnoc na nGall – hill of the foreigners
Townland: Ballyclogh
Barony: Pubblebrien
OS Sheet 65 in the area of 575 517

Ballyclough Castle is situated about 7 kilometres south of Limerick city centre close to the R511. A. Curry in 1840 stated that Ballyclough House was built on the site of an old castle and that part of the wall, about 3.5 metres thick, was incorporated at the north wall of the house.

Ballyclogh Castle 2
Parish: Lismakery
Townland: Ballyclogh
Barony: Connello
OS Sheet 64 ref area of 310 483

A later mansion or large house was built on the site. This castle was first mentioned in 1289 when it was in the possession of John and Roger Belcoe. In that same year it was granted to Maurice De Lacy. This castle was held by Edmond Og Lacy in 1580. He was killed, while hiding in the church of Knockpatrick, for his part in the Desmond Rebellion. The castle and lands were forfeited and given to an Elizabethan undertaker called William Trenchard. For a time after 1654, Nicholas Lillis, who paid rent to Colonel Strinchard, occupied it. By 1674 it was in the possession of one of the Boyle family, the Earl of Orrery, and left in the hands of a Colonel Simon Eaton.

Ballyculhaun (Ballyculhane) Castle
Parish: Kildimo / Cill Dama – church of St. Dima
Townland: Ballyculhane
Barony: Kenry
OS Sheet 65 ref 462 540
Situated near the mouth of the Maigue River about 2 kilometres northeast of Kildimo New.

This castle was surrounded by a 9-metre moat that was fed by a stream. It had a strong fortification or bawn measuring about 63 metres square with walls of over 10 metres in height and strengthened by towers at each corner. The castle itself measured 9 metres by 6 metres and had three storeys. The walls were over 1.25 metres thick.

It was an extremely safe place for the inhabitants but also for their animals. The towers or turrets contained small vaulted chambers and spiral stairways. On the south and southwest walls are windows and fireplaces indicating a previous two-storey building. During the reign of Elizabeth the castle was attacked and after a fierce battle one of the walls was breached and all those within were slaughtered to the number of one hundred and fifty, including women and children.

In the year 1581 it is stated that two bodies of troops left Adare to ravage the lands along the Maigue River. Having come together near Ballycahane they were attacked by a force under the command of David Barry of the Lake (probably Beach Lough) and were almost wiped out. When news of the defeat arrived at Adare an army was gathered and set out to take vengeance. David Barry, who was in the castle, was lucky to escape but was later captured on Scattery Island by the Mac Mahons of Clare and handed over to the English. He was later executed in Limerick, even though the castle of Ballycahane was in the possession of the Purcell family, who were devoted Loyalists at the time the massacre took place.

Ballycullen Castle
Parish: Lismakery
Townland: Ballycullen
Barony: Connello
OS Sheet 64 ref area of 322 492
Situated about 2 kilometres southwest of the town of Askeaton.

The site was later occupied by Ballycullen House. There are no remains. First referred to in the year 1289 when John and Roger Belcoe were in possession and in that same year it was granted to Maurice De Lacy.

David Fitzjames was the owner in 1581. He was killed

in the Desmond Rebellion. His son, called John, held the castle and lands until his death in 1616. His grandson, also called John paid rent to the Berkleys of Askeaton. In 1655 the Fitzjameses, who were also known as Nash, still held on, despite the fact that the lands had passed over to Lord Broghill. The Nashs still continued to hold on to the lands almost up to the early part of the twentieth century. James Nash had served under Lord Broghill and after losing a limb was incapacitated as a result. It may be interesting to note that James Nash had a son called Patrick. He married a Susan Carroll. Their son, called Carroll Nash, married into the Pierce family and in turn had a son called Patrick.

Ballyegan Castle / Castle Egney
Parish: Rathronan: Raith Ronan – fort of St. Ronan
Townland: Ballyegan
Barony: Shanid division of Connello
OS Sheet 64 near 280 415
Located close to Ballyvoghan Castle, and to Ballyegnybeg, and about 4 kilometres north of Ardagh.

A slender square tower not far from the nineteenth-century catholic chapel, this castle was almost the same as Ballyvaughaun and in about the same condition in 1840. It measured about 8 metres by 6.5 metres on the inside. The walls were 2 metres in thickness and what remained were just over 6 metres high.

Ballyegnybeg Castle
Parish: Cloonagh: Cluain Each – meadow of horses
Townland: Ballyegnybeg
Barony: Connello
OS Sheet 64 ref 282 421

Castle is situated about 3 kilometres north of Ardagh where there are the remains of a rectangular castle with walls of about 20 feet high. Part of a spiral stairway remains which is in good condition and runs to the top.
　See also Ballyvaughan and Ballyegan.

Ballyengland Castle
Parish: Askeaton
Townland: Ballyengland Upper
Barony: Lower Connello
OS Sheet 64 ref 372 498
3 kilometres east of Askeaton and 1 kilometre south of the N69.

Also known as Castle Hewson, this property once belonged to Keynsham Abbey. It was a fortified tower with outworks. In 1581 it was held by T. England whose son was hanged for rebellion. Around 1700 the castle came into the possession of the Hewsons.

Ballygleaghan Castle
Parish: Kilcornan
Townland: Curragh Chase North

Barony: Kenry
OS Sheet 65 ref 407 513
6 kilometres east of Askeaton and 3.5 kilometres south of Pallaskenry.

There are numerous spellings for this site and it is probably synonymous with Baile-Ui-Geilachain Castle.

This strong peel tower in a square court with turrets at each corner was reported to be in good repair in the 1730s but it must have been rebuilt or repaired because it had been, at least partially, destroyed by its Geraldine garrison in 1580. These Geraldines had withdrawn here after the fall of Carrigfoyle Castle. (See The Castles Of The Kingdom Of Kerry by Michael Carroll.) They preferred to slight the castle rather than it allowing it to be taken by Sir Nicholas Malby on his return eastwards after the destruction of Carrigafoyle Castle.

See also Derreen Castle.

Ballygrennan Castle 1
Parish: Owregare
Townland: Ballygrennan
Barony: Small County
OS Sheet 65 ref 634 350
This castle is situated about 1.5 kilometres south of Bruff, on the road to Kilmallock.

It was described as a late-sixteenth-century tower house over 16.5 metres high with embattlements. It is said that it had two tower houses – one of which may have been from the sixteenth century. There were two high gabled and chimneyed houses of a later date. Also, it had two large courtyards or bawns and numerous outbuildings. Only its extensive ruins can now be seen.

The town of Bruff was founded by the Anglo-Normans to guard the passes through the Galtee and Ballahoura Mountains. According to sources, in the time of Henry III the De Lacys built a castle at Bruff and another close by at Ballygrennan. The De Lacys became allies to the Fitzgeralds and participated in the Desmonds' misfortunes. On 4th April 1600 Pierce De Lacy was defeated by troops from Kilmallock under Captain Slingsby. De Lacy lost 300 men in this encounter.

At the time of the Cromwellian confiscations it was occupied by the Fox family and was then transferred to the Evans family.

Ballygrennan (Ballygenan) Castle 2
Parish: Saint Munchin
Townland: Ballygrennan
Barony: Liberties of Limerick
OS Sheet 65 in the area of ref 555 595

This castle was situated north of the Shannon about 4 or 5 kilometres northwest of the city centre. In the ordnance survey notes of 1840 this is listed as the site of an old castle called Ballygenan, which, by that date, had been completely remodelled into a dwelling house.

Ballygubba Castle
Parish: Tankardstown

Ballygrennan Castle 1

Townland: ?
Barony: Coshma
OS Sheet 73 ref area of 585 290

Possibly another name for the Tankardstown Castle. This castle was shown on the mid-seventeenth Down Survey but not in any of the following survey maps. Local tradition placed the castle in Ballygubba South on the farm of one John Lynch. Situated not far from the walled town of Kilmallock.

Ballyguileataggle Castle
Parish: unknown
Townland: Ballyguileataggle
Barony: Connello
OS Sheet 65 ref 461 328
7 kilometres southeast from Ballingarry just to the north of the R 518.

Ballymacshaneboy Castle
Parish: Kilquan / Cill Chuain – church of St. Cuan
Townland: Ballymacshaneboy / Baile Mac Shean Buidhe
Barony: Coshlea
OS Sheet 73 ref 595 205

The castle was situated in the valley of the townland of Ballymacshaneboy about 1 kilometre northwest of the old church. Described by Lewis as an ancient mansion of the Hall family with nearby remains of extensive fortifications.

The castle was in ruins by 1840 when only part of an arch remained.

Ballynagarde Castle
Parish: Fedamore / Fiadh Damair – wood of Damar
Townland: Ballynagarde
Barony: Clanwilliam
OS Sheet 65 ref 618 472

Ballynagarde Castle belonged to the Burkes of Clanwilliam but was forfeited with the adjoining lands in the Cromwellian confiscation. It then came into the possession of the Croker family who built Ballinagarde House. It is probably safe to assume that the stones of the castle were used to build Ballinagarde House, so it is likely that the castle was situated nearby and, in fact, O'Donovan stated that the house was built on the site of the old castle.
See also Williamstown and Rockstown castles.

Ballynahinch (Ballinahinch) Castle
Parish: Knocklong / Cnoc Luinge – hill of the camp (or earlier, Druim Damhghaire)
Townland: Ballynahinch or Ballinvreena
Barony: Coshlea
OS Sheet 73 ref 707 281
4 kilometres south of Knocklong town.

Associated with the family of Clangibbon, this castle stood in the southern part of the townland a short distance from the ruined church of Ballynahinch

It measured about 14 metres by 7 metres. A winding stairway ascended to the top of the building on the north end. There were gables on the north and south side, both with chimneys, which were built with bricks inside and stones outside. The walls were about 10 metres high and about 2 metres thick.

All the windows are quadrangular. Castle was built of limestone blocks.

Ballynamona Castle
Parish: Ballynamona or Moorstown
Townland: ?
Barony: Small County
OS sheet 65 in the area of 690 380
A castle built by the Raleighs in the reign of Elizabeth.

It is now lost but we can get an idea of its probable position. Lewis describes it as close to the road from hospital to Pallas green and on the banks of a stream.

Ballynamona townland is 4 kilometres north of Hospital on the R513 and a little to the south of this is Castlefarm.

Ballynoe Castle 1
Parish: Bruree
Townland: Ballynoe
Barony: Connello
OS Sheet 73 ref 550 290

This is another De Lacy castle. The castle is situated on high ground about 1 kilometre south of Bruree on the location of an old graveyard overlooking the village of Bruree and the river Maigue. It was described as a single peel tower built to guard the ford of the river beneath. The castle is about 21 metres high and the walls are about 1.7 metres thick.

It consists of five storeys with the third vaulted. It also has a spiral stairway.

The castle is now covered with ivy and in a dangerous condition. Almost adjoining the castle is the early medieval church of St. Mainchin, or Munchin. According to Westropp there is a strong tradition in the locality that the castle was built by the Knights Templars.

The castle was captured and almost destroyed in 1569 by the Elizabethan forces under the command of Captain John Warde during the rebellion of the Munster Geraldines.

Ballynoe Castle 2
Parish: Cloonelty / Cluain Eilte – meadow of the Doe
Townland: Ballynoe
Barony: Upper Connello
OS Sheet 64 ref 353 325
7 kilometres east of Newcastle West.

Described by Lewis as a castle built by the Knights Templar. It is close to the remains of a seventh-century church.

Note: This is not to be confused with the previously mentioned Ballynoe Castle. Despite the similarity in the references to a supposed Templar connection they are in fact separate places. Ballynoe is a very common townland name in County Limerick.

Ballysheedy Castle / Tower House
Townland: Ballysheedy
OS Sheet 65 ref 585 535
R511 5 kilometres south of Limerick city centre.

There is no information on the exact site of this castle but it was somewhere in the Roxborough area. It was in the possession of a James Fox in 1607.

Ballysiward (Howardstown) Castle
Parish: Unknown, possibly Bruree
Townland:
Barony: Coshma?
OS Sheet 65 in the area of 535 327

Situated north of Bruree in a place earlier known as Ballysyward or Ballysiward. Siward or Syward happens to have been a Norse name.

It appears that Homo de Valoignes had some claim to the land in the second half of the thirteenth century, but as recompense for damage to the church in Dublin when he was Justiciary of Ireland he lost ownership to Archbishop John Comin of Dublin.

The lands were passed on to a John de Auno and his heirs c. 1284 by Archbishop John Soundford of Dublin. In time the name de Auno changed to Dundon and that family held on to those lands from 1284 to about 1655. There is mention that this family had a manor house at Kilbreedy. Whether this was a house or tower house is open to question. It is noted that Ballysiward, which was in the King's possession in 1395, was granted to a Peter Fitzwilliam

Daundon/Dundon to hold in possession as 'to the King's wishes'.

During the Cromwellian Confiscation all the Dundon lands – which comprised about 1,000 acres and were located in the Barony of Small County – were divided amongst Cromwellian officers and soldiers by way of payment for services rendered. All the other lands in this general area belonging to the Earls of Desmond were earlier confiscated after the Geraldine Rebellion and given to George Bouchier.

Ballysteen Castle
Parish: Iverus
Townland: Ballinvoher
Barony: Kenry
OS Sheet 64 somewhere in the area of ref 354 563
North of Ballysteen village, close to Beagh Castle.

This castle belonged to the Dundon family until they were dispossessed in the sixteenth century. It was referred to by O'Donovan who relates that no trace remained in his time.

Ballytrasna (Bullytarsna) Castle
Parish: Grean / Grian – sun (sunny place)
Townland: Ballytrasna
Barony: Coonagh
OS Sheet 65 ref 739 448
2.25 kilometres northwest of old Pallas Grean.

A castle said to have belonged to the O'Briens existed here. In this area the foundation stones and some low parts of walls was to be seen in 1840.

The castle measured about 18 metres by about 6.5 metres.

Ballyvoghan Castle
Parish: Rathronan / Rath Ronain – fort of St Ronan
Townland: Ballyvoughaun / Baile Ui Bhuadhachain – town of the Vaughans
Barony: Shanid
OS Sheet 64 ref 277 407
2.5 kilometres north of Ardagh

This castle was in ruins in 1840. Nothing remained above 6 metres. It measured about 8 metres by 6 metres on the inside. The arch over the ground floor was still visible at that time.

See Ballyegnybeg.

Ballyvorneen Castle
Parish: Caherconlish
Townland: Ballyvorneen
Barony: Clanwilliam
OS Sheet 65 700 469
2.5 kilometres southeast of Caherconlish.

In 1655, Conor Clancie held this castle. It was a strong tower house with a large gabled wing attached. A nineteenth-century house was built on the site.

Ballywilliam Castle
Parish: Rathkeale / Rath Gaela
Townland: Ballywilliam West
Barony: Connello Lower
OS Sheet 64 in the area of 375 405
Aproximately 1.5 kilometres southeast of Rathkeale town.

When the area was inspected for the ordnance survey in 1840 little remained of this castle except for a heap of rubble and stones.

Beagh Castle
Parish: Iverus
Townland: Beagh
Barony: Kenry
Beagh: Betheach – the place of birch trees (also called Beahy)
OS Sheet 64 ref 357 569
On the bank of the Shannon estuary 2 kilometres north of Ballysteen.

The castle is built on a slight elevation of rock. The location is reputed to have been a former site of a Viking fort. In this context, Lewis related how a Viking prince disembarked here on his way up the Shannon. This prince was later converted to Christianity and when he returned to Beagh in 824 he built a church not far from the site of the castle.

The castle ruins are over 13 metres high. There is a good corbelled roof in the ground floor chamber as well as a spiral stairway. Sometime in the later half of the nineteenth century many dressed stones at the gables, the doors and windows were hacked away and removed. O'Donovan in 1840s refers to the castle 'as a rectangular building, three storeys high'. The walls were then standing and in good condition. A few steps of the spiral stairway were missing but access to the top was still possible.

The stone castle was built by the Fitzgeralds sometime in the thirteenth century, as the site was in a strategic location against raids from Thomond. In 1260, Beagh Castle was listed as one of the main fortifications of the Knight of Glin in the barony of Kenry. The castle has a large bawn. It is not known whether the existing ruins are those of the original castle or a later building. During its early existence the castle was the manor of the bishops of Limerick and was held by Richard and Lucy de Stakepole at the end of thirteenth century.

During the Plantation of Munster the castle and other lands of the Knight of Glin were transferred to George Beston and Lancelot Bostoche, who were both English undertakers. In 1598 the castle and lands again became the property of the Geraldines during the rebellion of the 'Sugan' Earl.

Beagh was the property of the Waller family from 1655 when Sir Hardress received it for services rendered to the Commonwealth. The castle was reputed to have been in ruins at this time. During the Napoleonic Wars, Beagh Castle was repaired and a vaulted embracement for a battery of guns was built on the western side reaching the first floor.

There are many stories about Beagh Castle, one of which was passed down in tradition. It relates that, in ancient times, the chieftain occupying the castle had a daughter named Emir, who had a lover called O'Kelly, whom her father detested. One night when the father returned unexpectedly and found the suitor in his daughter's chamber

Beagh Castle

he killed him. The daughter was so overcome with grief that she ran to the rocks by the Shannon and jumped into the river and drowned herself.

Local tradition also tells of the hidden treasure buried in Beagh Castle. It was based on the tale that a local woman had a recurring dream about buried treasure on many consecutive nights. When the other locals heard about this a number of men decided to dig for the treasure. They started digging one night at 10 pm and did not finish until 5 am the next morning. It is reported that no treasure was found but that they did encounter some skeletons.

Another version of this story is that, when a Danish ship was coming up the Shannon, the captain pointed to Beagh Castle saying that he had a map indicating where the old Danish treasures dating from Norse invasions were buried near the castle.

Black Castle 1
Parish: Knockainy / Cnoc Áine – Áine's Hill
Townland: Unknown
Barony: Small County
OS Sheet 645 405

The name Áine is taken from Lady Áine, daughter of Eogabhail, who is said to haunt the hill as a banshee. She is reputed to have been the second most famous banshee in Munster, after Eevil of Craglea in Thomond. She was mentioned very often by the Munster Bards in their elegies.

At the foot of Knockadoon Hill, at the south side of Loch Gur Lake, are the ruins of a castle which is called the 'Black Castle'. In 1840 it was but a ruin. On examination of the ruins it was found that the original square tower castle measured inside about 8 by 4.25 metres. The arch over the ground floor and part of the south wall to a height of about 10 metres still remained. The other three walls stood at an approximate height of 4 metres. The walls were 2.25 metres thick.

Now the castle is totally in ruins and little remains except a section of curtain wall with a gateway in the middle giving access to a promontory. A gateway on the wall, a short distance east of the tower, leads to a road to the great castle of Loch Gur. This castle was built by the Fitzgeralds in the fourteenth century and, together with the nearby Doon Castle (Bouchier's), it guarded the approach to Knockadoon.

Lough Gur gave title to the Fane family. Charles Fane of Basildon was a cadet of the Earl of Westmoreland's family. He was created Baron of Lough Gur in 1718 and Viscount Fane. His only son, Charles, died without issue in 1782 and his lands were left to his sisters' descendants – Mary, who had married Jerome Count De Salis in Switzerland, and Dorothy, who had married John, the Earl of Sandwich.

On Garrod's Island in the lake are traces of a building said to have been a castle of Gearoid, the fourth Earl of Desmond. Westropp describes this as a doubtful site but it is marked on the modern ordnance survey maps, sheet 65 ref 649 408.

Tales about Lough Gur – The Enchanted Lake
Every seven years the lake appears as if it completely dries out and a tree with a green cloth in its branches can be seen in the centre. One day when the lake dried out a man on horseback happened to be passing. He rode his horse to the centre and grabbed the fairy green cloth and then fled for his life. However, there was an old woman knitting under the cloth at the foot of the tree and, when she saw what was happening, she shouted out:

'Awake, awake, thou silent tide'
'From the Dead Woman's Land a horseman rides'
'From my head the green cloth snatching'

Immediately, the water rose in the centre and pursued the rider. As he gained the edge of the lake the water swept one half of his horse away with the green cloth that was flowing behind. Thus the enchantment was saved and still continues.

Many stories were told about Gearoid Iarla, Gerald, the fourth Earl of Desmond, who died in his castle at Newcastle in 1399. It is said that he used to dabble in magic.

At a feast in his castle he was asked to demonstrate his powers. He agreed but on the condition that no one should express their surprise. He then jumped in and then out of a bottle on the table. His father, however, could not control his amazement and immediately Gerald departed and made his way to the bank of the river Camogue and stepped into the water. He was immediately transformed into a goose and swam out of sight. It is said that he took up his abode on the island known as Gearoid's Island on Lough Gur and he then became known as the Goose of the Island.

Another story is that Gearoid, every seventh year since his death, rides a white steed with silver shoes across Lough Gur. Only when the silver shoes wear out will he be released from the spell. And, finally, there is the tale that Gearoid and his trusted men lie sleeping in a hidden cave on Knockadoon. They are all wearing their suits of armour and are lying down alongside their horses. When the right times arrives, they will all wake up from their magic spell and ride forth to free Ireland.

See also Bouchier's Castle.

Beagh Castle

Bouchier's Castle

Black Castle 2
Parish: Caherelly / Cathair Eillidhe – fort of Ailleach
Townland: Caherelly east
Barony: Clan William
OS Sheet 65 ref 666 445 gives the approximate area

Nothing remained of this castle in 1840. Lewis writing in the 1830s states that it had only recently collapsed.

The Hynes family of Caherelly is also mentioned by Fitzgerald regarding this castle.

See also in this area Caherelly Castle and Ballybricken Castle.

Bolane Castle / Beolaun Castle
Parish: Kildimo / Cill Dioma – church of St. Dima
Townland: Beolaun
Barony: Kenry
OS Sheet 65 ref 443 533
3 kilometres southeast of Pallas Kenry.

This tall square tower on the side of a steep ridge, near the village of Bolane, is thought to have been built by the O'Donovans in the fifteenth century.

This castle is somewhat similar to Ballycahane Castle. The keep occupies the west corner upon a rock that is some 6 metres higher than the adjoining level. One wall has been destroyed and parts are strewn everywhere. Alongside the keep is a round tower with a spiral stairway which opens on the level ground by a small door. This might have been a means of escape or else for drawing water from the nearby stream.

This castle, amongst others, was captured with cannon fire by Sir Hardress Waller in 1650.

Bouchier's Castle
Parish: Knockainy
Townland Knockadoon
Barony: Small County
OS Sheet 65 ref 648 410

Knockadoon or Bouchier's Castle is situated at the base of Knockadoon Hill, but on the northeast side of the lake.

The castle is in a good state of preservation. Described as a peel tower of about 25 metres in height, it measures about 16.5 metres by 10.5 metres on the outside base. A pistol loop overlooks the main entrance. It seems that the castle was built in two stages with the main almost square block added later.

Built by the Fitzgeralds in the fourteenth century, on the shore of Lough Gur. Along with Black Castle, it defended the two entrances to Knockadoon, a lofty eminence almost surrounded by the lake. On the summit of Knockadoon are traces of an ancient fortification. A later Doon Castle was erected on the site of the original by Sir George Bouchier, in the reign of James I.

In 1571, Gerald, the fifteenth Earl, and his brother John were imprisoned in the Tower of London for four years. On their release they returned to Lough Gur Castle where they threw off their English garb and reverted to the Irish native dress. In 1583, on the overthrow of the Geraldines and the death of Gerald, Lough Gur was granted to Sir G. Bouchier and his family continued to live there until 1641. The Bouchiers were the Earls of Bath in England.

Most of the historians state that this castle was built by Sir George Bouchier, son to the second Earl of Bath, during the reign of Elizabeth, when the Desmond properties were forfeited. However, this is very much in question as the stone and mortar used are the same as in the Black Castle, which would make its construction much earlier. With the change of the level of the waters in the lake it was most important that the Desmonds had a better fortification than the Black Castle. It is possible that Diarmuid Iarla built it, despite the fact that Carew only mentions one castle at Lough Gur. If the Black Castle were in a ruinous state at that time he would have disregarded mentioning it.

Lough Gur gave title to the Fane family. Charles Fane of Basildon was a cadet of the Earl of Westmoreland's family. He was created Baron of Lough Gur in 1718 and Viscount Fane. His only son, Charles, died without issue in 1782 and his lands were left to his sisters' descendants – Mary, who had married Jerome Count De Salis in Switzerland and Dorothy who had married John, the Earl of Sandwich.

On Garrod's Island in the lake are traces of a building said to have been a castle of Gearoid, the fourth Earl of Desmond. Westropp describes this as a doubtful site but it is marked on the modern ordnance survey maps, sheet 65 ref 649 408.

About a mile north of the town of Knockainy, a hospital or Commandery of the Knights Templar was located. Some walls and monument remained in 1840.

See also in this area, Knockaney, Black Castle, Kilballyowen, Baggotstown.

See Black Castle for history of Áine.

Brickfield (Kilbigly) Castle
Parish: Effin / Cill Eifinn – church of St. Eifinn
Townland: Brickfield
Barony: Coshlea
OS Sheet 73 In the area of ref 599 220
6.5 kilometres south of Kilmallock

The ruins of this castle were visible at the southwest of the townland.
  Only portions of the west, north and south wall remained in 1840. The highest part of the walls measured about 16.5 metres high and the thickness of the walls was about 2 metres.

Brittas Castle
Parish: Cahirconlish
Townland: Unknown
Barony: Clanwilliam
OS Sheet 65 ref 722 507

The castle was situated on the banks of the Mulkear River between Castleconnell and Limerick near Brittas Bridge. It is not known when the castle was built, but from the ruined walls and keep, it could be considered a strong edifice. There was one rounded corner tower or turret some 8 metres in diameter with a dome vault and the addition of a later latrine turret. It is said that a James Harrington from West Cork designed this new type of latrine with running water fed from an overhead stone container. There was also a wall extending to the river, plus another along the riverbank.

This castle was the chief stronghold of the Bourkes on the eastern part of their territory. This branch of the Bourkes was descended from Richard, the younger brother of the first lord of Castleconnell. Richard married the daughter of O'Mulrian of the adjoining barony of Owney. Their eldest son John married Grace, daughter of Sir John Thornton, treasurer of the English army in Munster. Refusing to submit to the Queen, his lands, crops, houses and one of his castles (Caherelly) were burned by Sir George Carew. He later was obliged to seek forgiveness on his knees in front of Sir George.

During the following four years, John lived at Brittas Castle. In 1603, having refused to take the oath of supremacy Sir John was imprisoned in Dublin Castle, but sometime later was allowed to return home. When a law was passed against harbouring priests, Sir John refused to surrender those priests who had sought refuge in his castles. He was then charged with treason and his castle was besieged. About fifteen days into the siege Sir John and some five of his followers escaped from the castle and made their way to Waterford. Sir John was captured and, still refusing to take the oath, was charged with treason and taken back to Limerick where he was hanged in 1607.

Broghill Castle
Parish: Colmanswell
Townland: Broghill North?
Barony: Connello Upper
OS Sheet 73 In the area of ref 523 245
Just to the northwest of Charleville.

It appears that after the Desmond Rebellion, the Earl of Desmond forfeited this property and it somehow came into the hands of Lord Broghill, i.e. Richard Boyle, first Earl of Orrery, who founded the town of Charleville. He was also known as the Earl of Cork. In 1641 he passed on ownership of the castle at Colmanswell and its lands to his son, Roger, on the occasion of his wedding. Roger had been previously knighted and given the title Baron Broghill.

See also Creggane Castle.

Bruff Castle
Parish: Bruff
Townland: unknown
Barony: Coshma
OS Sheet 65 ref 628 365

At the time of Henry III, the De Laceys built a castle at Bruff and another closeby at Ballygrennan.

The De Lacys became tributary to the Fitzgeralds and participated in the Desmond's misfortunes. On 4th April 1600 Pierce De Lacy was defeated by troops from Kilmallock under Captain Slingsby. De Lacy lost 300 men in this encounter.

Note: To the northwest of the town is Templebodean or Templeen, founded around 1284 by the Knights Templar.

See also Ballygrennan.

Bruree (Upper Lotteragh) Castle
Parish: Bruree / Brughrigh – fort of the kings

Townland: Upper Lotteragh
Barony: Upper Connello
OS Sheet 65 ref 549 403
7 kilometres north of Charleville.

This castle, which was called Upper Bruree, is situated in the burial ground besides the village. It was an almost square tower measuring at its base some 8 metres by 10 metres. Its walls were 1.75 metres thick and it had five storeys. It is reputed that this castle was built by O'Donovan but more likely erected by the De Lacys who were related to those of Ballingarry.

Lewis, however, says that it was a large and strong castle erected by the Templars in the twelfth century. They also had a church called Temple Colman or Cooleen.

Bruree was in earlier times the seat of the Kings of Munster. An Oilioll Ollum is said to have lived here in the second century. There were a number of ring forts and the outlines can still be seen, especially the one at Lotteragh Lower, which was called Lisoleem for Lios Oilioll Olluim. This was the place where the chief of the Hy-Figeinte resided. During the reign of Brian Boru the Fiacha Figeinte changed their name to O'Donovan (Dubhan/dark-haired man).

Bruree (Lower Lotteragh) Castle
Parish: Bruree / Brughrigh – fort of the kings
Townland: Lower Lotteragh
Barony: Upper Connello
OS Sheet 65 ref 543 311

Upper Lotteragh Castle, Bruree

The castle referred to as Lower Bruree is more of a fortress than a castle, as it has a strong high circular curtain wall which is about 50 metres in diameter and 1.75 metres in thickness. The highest part of the wall in 1840 was just over 8 metres. Within the wall there were three towers, with the one on the east side in a fair state in 1840. The other two, on the north and south sides were almost totally destroyed.

The one in fair condition was over 20 metres in height, with a footprint of about 6.3 × 7 metres. The main circular wall of the enclosure forms its east side to a height of about 6.5 metres. The tower had at least five storeys and was entered from the outside by a pointed strong doorway, which measured over 2 metres in height and about 1.6 metres in width. In the interior it is possible to observe an arch high up on the fourth floor. The intermediate timber floors have long disappeared. This tower was built of cut stone blocks, as were the other two where smaller blocks were used, indicating a later date of construction.

O'Donovan stated that the main wall, which resembles some others in the country, could have been built by the O'Donovans prior to 1178 when the O'Donovans were driven out of their territory by the Dal Cais.

Westropp writing much later says, referring to two towers and the bawn, 'the castle stands, like the forts, on the edge of the table-land on a steep bank of the Maigue river. The gate tower (misnamed O'Donovan's prison?) is still in fair condition. The outer gate is chamfered and recessed with a pointed arch, shot holes to the left and at the top blocks. The bawn of the castle is stated to be of earlier construction than the three towers. The retaining wall was built of large gritstone blocks and was D-shaped in plan. The wall was 1.8 metres thick with an average height of about 4 metres. The gateway was 2.4 metres high and 1.5 metres wide with a porter's lodge on the right. Over the porch are two chambers resting on corbels.

Westropp also wrote that the second tower that existed during his visit was about 8 metres by 5.5 metres and lower than the other tower. It had a broken stairway, a small bartizan on the northwest corner; the top storey built over a large vault and had two small vaulted cells in the basement. The third tower no longer existed.

It is reputed that this castle was built by O'Donovan, King of Bruree, who was later dispossessed by the De Lacys.

Sometime after 1200, Hamo de Valoignes, King John's representative, granted Bruree and the land around it, to John de Mareys (de Marisco) and his wife Mabel, who happened to be Hamo's daughter. This was a marriage gift. John was a son of Geoffrey de Marisco who found himself in dire trouble with both the Church and Crown. All the Marisco lands were confiscated and Bruree was included. After John's death in 1242 his wife regained the Bruree lands. These lands were passed on to Robert de Marisco, the son, who later passed them on to Maurice De Lacy and his wife Eve, who was Robert's daughter. It appears that the De Lacys were first known as de l'Esse, de Lesse or de Lees. The De Lacy name, as such, only came into being late in the 1500s. In 1320, a Patrick De Lacy held Bruree and after his death his wife, Dervala, sued Maurice Fitzpatrick De Lacy for her dower in her late husband's manor. Maurice had three sons and it seems that the third son, called Odo, became the heir, as well as sheriff of Limerick. A loyal follower of the Earl of Desmond, as well as being underlord, he was killed in a skirmish in 1412 at Kilmallock.

The De Lacys lost all their possession following the Cromwellian settlement. They lost Bruree, Garroose, Gerrane, Lisinchonna, Ballyfookeen, Ballinwillin and Balinoran, This was a total of some 2,500 acres of land which were taken over by Sir Charles Lloyd and these were later passed onto the adventurer Samuel Avery.

At the conclusion of the Jacobite–Williamite War (1689 to 1691) most of east Limerick County was held by the Williamite forces. At Athlacca, Captain John Odell of Ballingarry had a strong force of dragoons for the defence of the general area.

Not too far away, at Newcastle and Gort na Tiobraide, the Jacobite forces were located and from here they raided into the lands held by the Williamite forces and burned the towns of Ballingarry and Bruree. The ancient castle of Ballynoe was already in ruins at this time, as well as most of the De Lacy castles following the Cromwellian conquest. During this time of conflict a Colonel Pierce Lacy defeated the Williamite forces under Captain John Odell near Athlacca. In that same year we have a Pierce Edmond De Lacy and his thirteen-year-old son, Peter De Lacy, mentioned in the defence of Limerick Castle. After the signing of the Treaty of Limerick, Pierce Edmond with his sons left Ireland with Sarsfield and they all had outstanding military careers in Europe where they all rose to Field Marshall or higher in the various European armies.

The main castle, which was referred to as 'the Manor' was burned and destroyed in 1691, it was called the 'Lower' De Lacy Castle to distinguish it from the other De Lacy Castle built on high ground near Bruree.

Nearby a castellated building erected by the Knights Templars was situated near Lisoleem. (*This might refer to other Bruree Castle.*)

Bulgaden Castle
Parish: Kilbreedy Major / Cill Bhrighde – church of St. Bridget
Townland: Bulgaden
Barony: Coshma
OS sheet 65 ref 642 303
5.5 kilometres northeast of Kilmallock

The ruins of the castle measured 7.5 by 5.8 metres on the inside. There were two doorways on the south wall.
The walls were 2.25 metres thick and only one floor with an arch underneath remains.

Cahernarry Castle
Parish: Cahernarry
Townland: Unknown

This castle or tower house was situated in Roxborough area. Somewhere near OS Sheet 65 ref 588 515.
The site is not known today. All that is known is that this castle was one of those belonging to the Burkes of Clanwilliam.

Caherconlish Castle
Parish: Cahirconlish / Cahir Chinn Lis / Caherconlish / Cathair Chinn Lis – stone fort near the Lis
Barony: Clanwilliam
OS Sheet 65 ref 680 494

It is said that the de Burgos built a strong stone castle at this location on the site of an ancient Irish fort.

It is stated by Fitzgerald that Caherconlish was a strong walled town built and defended by four nearby castles and was similar to the town of Kilmallock. The town was walled in 1358 at the expence of those traders who came through on their way to Limerick. The castles were not built into the walls like Kilmallock but were within a radius of a mile or so. Within the walls was a college. A strong gateway and parts of this college were still to be seen c. 1826.

Lewis says that Cahirconlish House was erected on the site of a castle that belonged to the Wilson family. This castle collapsed without warning leaving only half of the former structure, including a gateway with the arms of the Wilson family.

On the night of 17th August 1690, King William III of England camped here on his way to Limerick. The exact location of the camp was in the townland of Boskill, just east of the main castle of Caherconlish.

During the second Williamite siege of Limerick, Ginkel's forces also camped here. Most of his soldiers died here from the plague, probably cholera. A large mound near the small river called the Groody River is supposed to have been the burial place. In later years, during digging, a mass of bones were encountered.

See also Carrigareely and Knockatancashlane.

Caherelly Old Castle
Parish: Caherelly / Cathair Eillidhe / Ailleach – fort of Ailleach (or Ballybricken)
Townland: Caherelly west
Barony: Clanwilliam

OS Sheet 65 ref 658 438
14 kilometres southeast of Limerick. 1.5 kilometres east of the R514 near the Camoge River.

The castle was situated not far from the old church in this townland. Built on high ground it measured about 7 metres square and stood over 20 metres high. It was in good condition with its roof still intact in 1840.

The Hynes family is said to have built this castle.

Cappagh Castle
Parish: Cappagh
Townland: Cappa
Barony: Lower Connello
OS Sheet 64 ref 390 452
7 kilometres southeast of Askeaton, 500 metres south of Cappagh cross.

The name signifies a level area laid out for tillage. The castle was built on a low rock and had a stone-walled court. It commanded one of the most important passes in the line of hills to the north.

It was over 23 metres high and the walls were over 1.6 metres thick. Only the north wall was standing in 1896. The castle had five floors and must have been a magnificent structure in its prime. This was originally a Fitzgerald, Desmond castle.

Held by Francis Morton, in 1642, it was surrendered to the Irish Confederate force. When the Irish forces took possession of Limerick Castle they also acquired a number of cannons. Now they had the means to attack the castles where the English had taken refuge. Amongst the cannons was a piece of some 404 kilo, which could shoot a ball of 14.5 kilo. This was probably the biggest cannon in Ireland at that time and had been mounted on Limerick Castle walls for defensive purposes. The only problem was that it lacked a carriage. Improvising, a huge tree was hollowed out and the gun was placed inside. This was pulled by twenty-five yoke of oxen over bogs, marshes, streams and rough terrain. With the arrival of this monstrosity near their walls, castle after castle surrendered. Cappagh opened its gates, Castle Matrix was yielded up, Askeaton surrendered and Kilfinny hung out a white flag after receiving four direct hits from the great cannon on 29th July 1642.

Cappagh Castle is reputed to have been blown up later by Sir Hardress Waller.

Carrickania / Carraig an Fhiaigh Castle
Parish: Kilcornan / Cill Chornain – church of St. Cornan
Townland: Ballyshonickbane
Barony: Kenry
OS Sheet 65 ref 410 540
On a minor road just south of Pallaskenry.

This castle is situation on a limestone rock which is surrounded by a bog making access almost impossible. The north and south walls still remained to a height of about eighteen feet but there was no trace of the other two walls. The distance between the two existing walls was only 5.25 metres giving the impression that this was a small tower house.

Carrick-Kital Castle
Parish: Kilteely / Kill-Teidhill
Townland: Carrickittle
Barony: Small County
OS Sheet 65 somewhere in the area of 745 397
2.5 kilometres southeast of Kilteely village.

It is reputed that it was built by the Lord Chief Justice of Ireland in the year 1510 according to the *Annals of the Four Masters*. The castle was shown on an engraved map from the Down Survey. But no remains have been visible for at least 160 years.

Note: It is reputed that the Knights Templars had a 'house' in this locality. This would probably mean a church and tower. No further details are recorded.

Carrigareely Castle
Also called O'Farrell's Rock or Carrigifariogla
Parish: Cahirconlish
Townland: Carrigareely
Barony: Clanwilliam
OS Sheet 65 ref 666 504
About 2 kilometres northwest of Cahirconlish.

Built by the Bourkes but last occupied by the O'Dalys. See also Cahirconlish and Knockatancashlane.

Carrigogunnel Castle
Parish: Kilkeedy

Townland: Carrigogunnel
Barony: Pubblebrien / Pola Ui Bhriain – O'Brien's country
OS Sheet 65 ref 498 553
Situated northwest of Mungret, near the little village of Clarina.

Earlier known as Carraigh O'Coinnell or Carraig O gConaing from the tribe of the O'Conaings who occupied the territory before the Normans.

Built on the summit of a great basaltic rock about 50 metres above the level of the Shannon. There is a ruined round tower which is 10 metres in diameter located at the north corner which could have been a keep or a corner tower to a large courtyard castle. West of the keep is a hexagonal room that is probably dated from the fourteenth century or maybe earlier. Further on is a substantial hall block with cellars and a passage descending to the ground floor. East of the round tower or turret is a four-storey tower house, possibly of the early fifteenth century which has an inner bawn or courtyard. The outer enclosure or bawn seems to have been heart shaped and measured about 75 metres in each direction. This bawn was surrounded by a wall to the east and the west but without flanking towers. The gateway is situated near a projection at the rounded south corner. Near or at the east corner there are the remains of some further buildings. According to Leask the greater parts of what remains today date from the fifteenth century.

Carraig Ui gConaing or Carrigogunnel, in the parish of Kilkeedy, was given by King John to Donncadh Cairbreach O'Brien, King of Thomond, in 1210, as Donald, his father, had been an ally of the Anglo-Normans and assisted them in establishing a base in Limerick. Sometime around 1377 the Earls of Desmond took over the castle when it was known

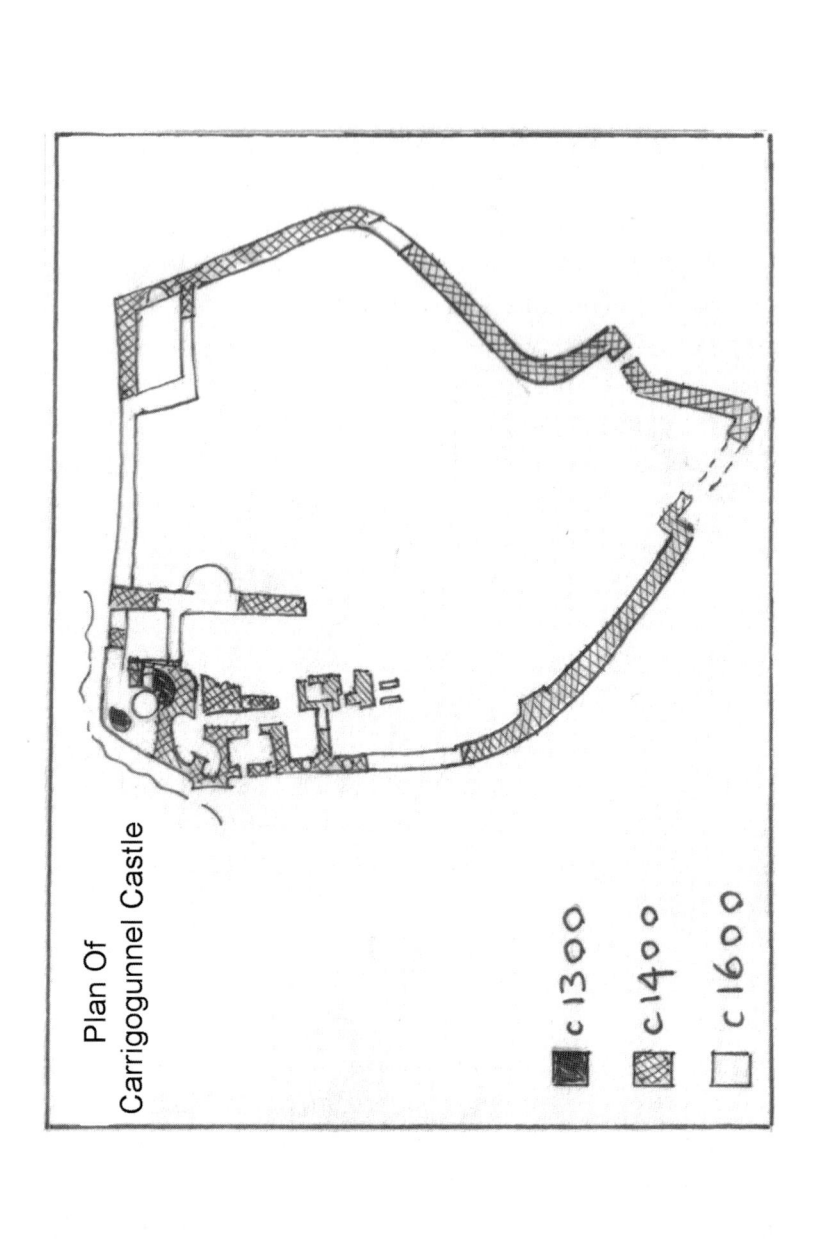

Plan Of
Carrigogunnel Castle

■ c 1300
▨ c 1400
☐ c 1600

as Carrig Gunning. The first castle has been ascribed to the Knights Templars. That castle was not taken over by the O'Briens until 1332 when the Templars were suppressed. They must have been in occupation for over a century.

The castle was intrinsically linked with the castle or manor of Esclone/Esclon (Aos Cluan in Irish) which preceded it. There are no records that show the exact site of Esclon or what it looked like. More than likely, it was built as a fosse, moat, and a timber fortification near the river Shannon. The name Esclon was replaced by 'Fossa Llymerey', which means wastelands or flooded lands. It is reputed that the name Esclon is of Norse extraction due to the fact that they built a number of forts in this area c.850 to 1150. About 1200 the area was in the hands of William de Burgo but some 14 years later reverted to King John.

In 1499, James Fitzgerald, Earl of Thomond, conferred the region of Esclon and most of the surrounding lands to Brian Duv O'Brien, who was in control of most of that region at that time. He was a descendant of Prince Teige Glemore O'Brien who had died in 1426. After this exchange, the region became known as Pubblebrien. Brien 'Duv' (black features), married Mary Mac Mahon from Clare and after this union Carrigogunnel became the chief residence of the O'Briens up to the time of the Cromwellian confiscations. Brian Duv gave aid to the English forces during the Desmond rebellion and laid waste the Barony of Kenry with his own forces. He formally surrendered his lands to Queen Elizabeth in June 1584 and in the regrant he obtained nearly the whole of the Barony of Pubblebrien. He died in 1615, and was succeeded by his only son, Donough, who took over the castle at Carrigogunnel in 1622. He married Margaret Thornton, daughter of Sir George Thornton, but they had no children. When Donough died his widow married

Edmond Burke, Lord of Castleconnell and when Edmond died in 1638, Margaret inherited parts of two vast estates. Following the death of Donough in 1632 that particular line of the O'Briens ceased and the castle and lands of Carrigogunnel passed over to another Donough, who happened to be the grandson of 'Mago'. He took the side of the Irish in the Uprising of 1641. He was accused of rebellion and his property was confiscated. These were not returned under the later Act of Settlement.

The castle of Carrigogunnel was confiscated after the Confederate wars but suffered no siege or attack. It was occupied by a Captain Wilson in 1651 but was taken over by Sir Hardress Waller, one of those who signed the death warrant of Charles I. Michael Boyle, who later became the archbishop of Dublin, was in control of the castle c. 1655 and had a John Caper in residence. In July 1666, the castle and lands were granted to Boyle under the Act of Settlement and remained in his possession until 1698. In the meantime Boyle gave a lease of the lands to a Thomas Monsell in 1692.

After the battle of Aughrim in 1691, when the Irish retreated to Limerick, the castle was held for King James. Following the second siege of Limerick, General Scravemore assaulted the castle and the garrison surrendered. It was then blown up to prevent it being held by the Irish. What can be seen today are the remnants from that event. Finally, it is interesting to note that in the confiscations of Carrigogunnel and the lands of Pubblebrien, the Duke of York accepted the grant of the confiscated lands of people such as the O'Briens, who would later perish in his service when he became James II.

Some say that the name of the place was Carraig Coinneal – the Rock of the Candle. It is said that a witch lived on the rock in olden times and that every evening at nightfall she lit the candle. Anybody who saw it died immediately. However, when St. Patrick blessed the well at Patrickswell some miles away, he said some prayers on behalf of the people and the light of the candle was extinguished forever.

Note: Lewis refers to a Carrig-a-Quincy in this area as a Templar castle that was later granted to the O'Briens. We have no other references but there are various townland names in the vicinity that might be suggestive of castle sites.

We have no other references but there are various townland names in the vicinity which might be suggestive of castle sites. Carrig west and east, Ballmacashel.

Castle Comfort
Parish: Abbington / Abbeyowny / Mainistir Uaithne – monastery of Uaithne
Townland: Fernane
Barony: Owneybeg
OS Sheet 65 ref 722 552
About 14 kilometres east of Limerick, and close to the village of Moroe.

This was the seat of the Rev. O'Brien Costelloe P.P. The house was built in 1824. The site was previously occupied by an old castle which fell into complete ruins. The castle was referred to as Castle Comfort!
See Abington.

Castleconnell Castle
(also known as Castle Connell / Caislean Ui Chonaill / Caislean Ui Chonaing / Caislean O gConaing – castle of the O'Conaings)

Parish: Stradbally / Sraid Baile – street town
Townland: Coolbawn
Barony: Clanwilliam
OS Sheet 58 ref 660 625
Close to the river in the South West of the town.

It is now very difficult to try and trace the details of the castle but it may be judged that the walls were about 53 metres long by 30 metres wide and had round towers on the western corners and possibly on the others. These towers were something similar to the towers of King John's Castle at Limerick. The castle compound had at least two halls. One was a building about 25.5 metres long, which was later at some stage subdivided. The other hall, known as Desmond's Hall, is almost complete with a vaulted basement. These halls had probably timber and thatched roofs originally.

Towards the end of the twelfth century Castleconnell passed into the hands of the O'Briens. Castleconnell was then but an earth-ramparted dun with timber fortifications. One of the stories told about this period was when King Donald Mor O'Brien, returning from the victory over the Anglo-Normans at Thurles, visited his uncle Dermot at Castleconnell. Leaving his army and escort across the Shannon he quietly accepted his uncle's hospitality, but in the dead of night part of his force crossed the Shannon and took possession of the fort. His uncle Dermot and Mahon, grandson of Brian Boru were attacked, seized, and their eyes plucked out. Mahon died immediately but Dermot lingered for a number of days. The fort was then occupied by Donald Mor, until Charles, the Red Handed, O'Connor defeated the O'Briens and took possession of Castleconnell in A.D. 1200.

The castle reverted to the O'Briens after a large ransom was paid for the release of Ulchin O'Brien and his wife.

King John in 1201 granted to William de Burgo the seat of Castleconnell provided that he fortified the castle and restored it to the king on demand while being recompensed for his loss.

Despite the fact that de Burgo married a daughter of Donal Mor O'Brien, King of Munster, the O'Briens had no intention of giving up this important region and, late in the year 1261, Brian Roe O'Brien burned and demolished the new castle after all the garrison had been killed. Having been regained it was reinforced and enlarged by Walter de Burgh in late 1290. One branch of the de Burgo became Barons of Castleconnell and it became the main seat of this family for the next five hundred years, with a brief exception when Donagh O'Brien with Edward Bruce came south and stayed at the castle during the Easter of 1316. Another branch became Barons of Brittas Castle.

The Burkes of Castleconnell and their relations, the Burkes of Brittas, were descended from Edmond de Burgh, the 'Red Earl' of Ulster. In the early Desmond wars the Burkes found themselves on the side of the Desmonds, as Sir William Burke, of Castleconnell, was married to Catherine, daughter of the fifteenth Earl of Desmond. In 1580, Queen Elizabeth rewarded the De Burghs for their loyalty to the Crown by creating William a peer of the Realm. This was poor reward for the loss of his two sons in a skirmish with James Fitzmaurice. William locked himself away in the castle and died some four years later.

John Burke, the second Earl of Castleconnell, while in London in 1592, got involved in a dispute with a Captain Arnold Cosby which lead to a duel. As Burke was about to dismount from his horse he was run through by Cosby and died on the spot. Cosby, as a result of his treachery, was condemned to death and hanged at the Tower. John was succeeded by his young brother, James, who became the third Lord Castleconnell.

During the Insurrection of 1641, William, the sixth Lord Castleconnell and his relation, Lord Brittas, joined the Confederates. They raised a regiment of cavalry each. After the failed uprising their lands were confiscated and granted to Sir Charles Coote. Lord Castleconnell fled to the continent where he served in the royal regiment of Charles I until after the Restoration when his lands were restored by Charles II.

During the war between William and James, the castle was occupied by the Jacobite forces but surrendered to the Prince of Hesse on 29th August 1691, after a short blockade. After the Battle of the Boyne, the eighth Lord Castleconnell went with James II to France where he died childless. In 1651 the castle was in the possession of the parliamentary forces and became a storehouse during the siege of Limerick, after being surrendered by a small Irish force. After William raised the siege of Limerick an attempt was made to blow up the castle but without success. The following year, on 28th August 1691, Ginkle brought five cannons and the castle was almost totally destroyed. Many of the garrison of some two hundred and fifty men were killed. With the almost utter destruction of the castle the title of Lord Castleconnell also expired. William Burke and his relations went to France with Sarsfield. The last of the Burkes died about one hundred years later fighting for France.

There is a curious story relating to the 'enchanted' Earl of Desmond contained in the Smith MSS where he takes on the form of a Black Horse in and around Castle Connell. In a letter sent to the Archbishop of Armagh the following is roughly quoted: 'There are reports of strange noises, sometimes of drums and trumpets, other times of strange music with heavenly voices, then terrible screaming and screeching, so much so that the local people cannot sleep at night. Priests have gone there but by some power have ended up miles away without explanation. On occasions infinite numbers of soldiers and horsemen have been seen. Some of these apparitions dance with a Mrs. Burke throughout the nights and try to entice her to come away with them to be the wife of the Lord of Desmond. On his return from a fair, a man encounters a gentleman who invites him into a castle and shows him a magnificent black horse lacking a fourth shoe, which he says is the Earl of Desmond. When the fourth shoe is fitted the horse will turn into the Earl again and many fighting men will accompany him out the gates. There was never a castle before or after in this location.'

Castle Oliver
Parish: Kilfinane
Townland: Castleoliver
Barony: Costlea
OS Sheet 73 ref 665 195
3.5 kilometres southwest of Kilfinane.

The original castle, built near the site of the present castellated mansion of 1849, has completely disappeared. This mansion replaced another older house.

The castle was associated with the Fitzharrises, then the Roches and finally the Olivers, who occupied the castle after 1641. They were Cromwellians who received large tracts of land following the Cromwellian plantation. A captain Charles Oliver was regarded as a tyrannical magistrate and a law unto himself, during the United Irishmen Uprising in 1798.

Castle Erkin
Parish: Caherconlish
Townland: Castle-erkin
Barony: Clanwilliam
OS Sheet 65 ref area of 708 488

There are various seventeenth-century references to this site in relation to the Burke family, and in 1604 Castle Erkin was held by J. Burke.
　No details of the structure survive.

Castlequarter Old Castle
Parish: Kilbehenny / Cill Beithne – church of the birch tree
Townland: Castlequarter
Barony: Coshlea
OS Sheet 74 ref 847 166
1.5 kilometres northwest of Kilbehenny Village.

It is said that this castle was built by Beithne O'Brien, who also built the church at Kilbehenny. Only the foundations of the south and west walls were visible in 1840. The castle measured internally about 8 metres by 15 metres. There were five storeys in total. The walls were about 1.25 metres thick and the height of the castle was about 19 metres.

Castle Rag
Parish: Ballingarry / Baile an Gharaidh – garden town
Townland: Rylaans
Barony: Upper Connello
OS Sheet 65 ref 414 362

This castle was situated near Ballingarry town. It was next to the Church of Ireland church in the townland of Rylaans, near a house owned by a Major Odell. Nearby there was an old religious house called the Priory. The field where some of the foundations have been found is called the 'Friary Field'. It is said that this priory belonged to the Knights Bannerets. Nearby in the same townland is situated a bastion or turret of an old castle said to have been occupied by the De Lacy family. It is known locally as 'the Turret'.

If all the above is true, it is a clear indication that the Templars and the De Lacys were friends and that they may have come to Ireland together.

See also Ballingarry Castle and Woodstock Castle.

Castle Roberts
Parish: Adare / Atha Dara – ford of the oak
Townland: Castle Roberts
Barony: Coshma
OS Sheet 65 ref 491 447
Very close to Fanningstown.

Castle Siward (Rathsiward)
Parish: Cahernarry
Townland: Uncertain
Barony: Clanwilliam
Possibly the castle site marked at OS Sheet 65 ref 631 534

Castle Troy
Parish: Kilmurry / Cill Mhuire – church of Mary
Townland: Castletroy

In the liberties of Limerick city
OS Sheet 65 ref 628 587
Situated east of Limerick city close to the National Technological Park.

The ruins of this castle are found on the south bank of the Shannon River. It gave its name to the townland. All that remained in 1840 were the east and north walls and some of the other two: 3 metres of the west wall and 2 metres of the south wall.

The castle measured at its inside base some 10 metres by 6.5 metres. The walls were 2 metres thick and the height of the castle was about 22 metres with five storeys that all contained windows.

This castle was built by the O'Briens in the time of Henry III c. 1260/1275 but seems to have been repaired and modified at a later stage – possibly in the 1600s.

Referred to as Callagh Itroy or Garraneightragh in the Down Survey.

Castle Guard

Parish: Doon
Townland: Castleguard
Barony: Coonagh
OS Sheet 65 ref 793 495
4 kilometres northeast from Pallas Green.

This castle was associated with the Desmonds but its history is unknown.

Castlejane
Parish: Knocklong
Townland: Unknown
Barony: Coshlea
OS Sheet 65 ref somewhere near 752 306

The only information we have on the above is an inscription on stone in a nearby graveyard saying that a monument was erected by William Ryves of Castlejane.

A bridge 300 metres east of the old burial ground is called Castle Jane Bridge. Ryves Castle is less than 1 kilometre to the south.

Whether this was a castle or a mansion, it existed prior to A.D. 1714. It was possibly a tower house of some kind. In the 1830s it was the residence of Thaddeus R. Ryan.

Castlemahon (Mahoonagh) Castle
(Castle Meine or Meine Castle)
Parish: Mahoonagh
Townland: Mahoonagh
Barony: Upper Connello
OS Sheet 64 ref 318 312
Situated in the Glenquin Division of the Barony of Upper Connello 5 kilometres southeast from Newcastlewest.

The castle stood about 300 metres from the old church. It measured about 11 metres by 8 metres on the inside. The walls were 2 metres in thickness and in 1840 stood to a height of 11 metres. Even though it was a strong castle there were no indications of arches. There were windows made of limestone blocks but these are now damaged.

In reference to this castle it is mentioned in Wilson's history that 'near Newcastle are the magnificent ruins of "Castle Maghan".' This no doubt refers to the above castle which must have been a large and imposing structure in its day. Nearby stood a circular building with a high conical roof of stone which may have been built by the Knights Templar, as they are reputed to have had a preceptory nearby at Ballynoe. Lewis refers to a Templar castle and ecclesiastical buildings at 'Mayne'.

This castle or tower house gives its name to the nearby village. Castlemahon was supposed to have been a strong fortress of the Fitzgeralds and had been built c. 1490, reputedly by Gibbon, the second son of Gilbert Fitzgibbon, who was related to Thomas Fitzgerald of Newcastle. The eldest son, Maurice, was knighted after the Battle of Halidon Hill in Scotland where the English defeated the Scots. Maurice had raised about 2,000 soldiers in Ireland to fight for the Crown. Maurice also acquired a reputation for 'gallantry and intrigue with the fair sex' and eventually married a woman by the name of Bruce in Scotland. It is uncertain if she was of that royal Scottish line. He then moved to England where a daughter married the youngest son of the Earl of Northumberland. In his later years he returned to his native domain and died soon after his arrival.

In the Desmond survey of 1584 the castle is described as being wealthy and spacious before it was destroyed in the Geraldine Rebellion. Nothing remained then, only stone walls, which can still be seen standing on a slight incline near the village of Mahoonagh.

In an unpublished Geraldine document it is said that 'In the fourth year of Queen Mary, John Oge Fitzgibbons, the White Knight, and his kinsmen David, Gilbert, and

Thomas, released unto James, Earl of Desmond, all their lands in Connello', i.e. the manors of Meane and Ballytine, the Short Castle at Askeaton, etc.

Castlematrix / Castle Matras
Parish: Rathkeale / Rath Gaela
Townland: Castlematrix
Barony: Connello Lower
OS Sheet 64 ref 352 412
This castle is near Rathkeale town, on the left bank of the Deel River and about 1.5 kilometres southwest of the town. About 400 metres to the east is Glebe Castle.

Castlematrix adjoins the Augustinian Priory, which is said to have been founded by Gilbert Harvey c. A.D. 1289. The castle itself measured 14 metres by 11.25 metres on the outside. The walls are 2 metres thick and the castle stands over 20 metres high. It consisted of four storeys – one vaulted and two above. Access to the upper rooms was by a spiral stairway in one corner which extended into a turret. The vaulted floor had collapsed and the floor fallen to the ground by 1840. Parts of the wall have also fallen. Only one part of the tower on the north side remained in 1890. This adjoining tower had four storeys in the main block and at the east wall had seven storeys. In addition it had another wing which was lower than the main tower and had three storeys. This seems to have been added at a later date.

This was the principal stronghold of the Geraldines in the Rathkeale district and is reputed to have been built c. 1440, but the name suggests that it had an earlier beginning and almost certainly a Templar connection.

Castlematrix was originally called Matres according to Colonel Sean O'Driscoll, who once occupied the castle. Castle Matres is a similar name to at least two locations in France – on the Seine and the Marne – where the Templars had establishments.

In ancient pagan times the Deel was a sacred river where the Matres were honoured. These were the goddesses of love, fertility and poetry and were later revered as a single person who became known as the Matrix.

James, the ninth Earl of Desmond, was murdered in this castle by his servants on 7th December 1487. Maurice, his brother and successor, apprehended all those who were involved and had them hanged.

In late October 1580, in the midst of the Geraldine Rebellion, Lord Grey, the Lord Deputy of Ireland arrived at the castle. Accompanying him were Edmund Spencer and the courtier, Walter Raleigh. After Lord Grey and the army had left for Dun-an-Oir in Kerry where a force of Italians, Spanish and Irish had landed, Raleigh stayed behind. When the local population of men women and children came to the camp site to see if there was any food left, they were slaughtered by Raleigh and a troop of English soldiers.

As a result of the Geraldine confiscations, Spencer and Raleigh were granted large estates which were left in the hands of one William Southwell. It is said that the potato was imported to Ireland by Raleigh and first planted around Rathkeale.

In 1610, the Jacobean wing of the castle was completed and it was thus transformed into a substantial residence.

In 1641 when the Irish forces took possession of Limerick Castle they also acquired a number of cannon. Now they had the means to attack the castles where the English had taken refuge. Amongst the cannons was a piece of some 404

Carrigogunnel Castle

Castle Matrix

kilo, which could shoot a ball of 14.5 kilo. This was probably the biggest cannon in Ireland at that time and had been mounted on Limerick Castle walls for defensive purposes. The only problem was that it lacked a carriage. Improvising, a huge tree was hollowed out and the gun was placed inside. This was pulled by twenty-five yoke of oxen over bogs, marshes, streams and rough terrain. With the arrival of this monstrosity near their walls, castle after castle surrendered. Cappagh opened its gates, Castle Matrix was yielded up, Askeaton surrendered and Kilfinny hung out a white flag after receiving four direct hits from the great cannon. Castle Matrix was fairly soon retaken by Cromwellian forces.

In 1642 an early English planter named Herbert killed a number of English colonists in Rathkeale town. He also burned the castle of Castlematrix. The village and castle at that time belonged to a Sir Thomas Southwell. In 1662 Thomas Southwell was created a baronet by King Charles II. He is known as the person who brought the Palatines to south Limerick c. 1700. These were Lutheran refugees who fled their lands because of religious persecution after the French invaded their homeland. About twelve hundred settled around Castle Matrix and the adjoining countryside. Even though many of these families stayed in the locality a good number from the following generations sailed for New England.

See also Rathkeale Castle and Glebe Castle.

Castletown Castle 1
Castletown Conyers / Castle Mac Eineiry
Parish: Castletown-Conyers / Corcomohide / Corca-Muiceat – McEniry's territory

Townland: Castletown
Barony: Upper Connello East
OS Sheet 73 ref 443 298

This ruined castle, built of brown sandstone, is situated about 1 kilometres south of the village of the same name. This village was in earlier times called 'Kilmoodan' but later took the name Castletown Mac Eineiry, after the castle which was erected in 1349 by a chief of that name. This family were the local chieftains of Corca Muichead and the area is also known as Corcamohide. The Mac Enirys held on to the castles and lands until c. 1641. It is also known as Castletown Conyers after an English settler family.

This was supposed to have been a fine castle but in 1840 only a small part of the ruins remained. These remains were located near a house of Mr. Coniers. The Mc Enirys were dispossessed by Cromwell c. 1650 and the land and castle passed to the Coniers family.

In the early seventeenth century the castle and lands were in the possession of Sir Hardress Waller who had married one of the daughters of Sir John Dowdall of Kilfinny Castle. He came to Ireland in the reign of Charles I, as a member of the Privy Council. On the capture of the castle by the Irish in the Insurrection of 1641 he retired to England and joined the Parliamentarians and rose to the rank of Major General. He was one of the judges in the so-called trial of Charles I. He was sent to Ireland in 1649 with eight hundred troops with the objective of destroying all the castles in Limerick which were in rebel hands. After the Restoration all his Irish estates were forfeited, but the Castle and lands at Castletown were saved, as they were the property of his wife who was a supporter of the Loyalists.

Castletown was besieged on 26th March 1642, by the Confederate Irish in a force of some four hundred men, under the command of Patrick Purcell of Croagh, Captain John Fitzgerald, the younger brother of the Knight of Glin, and lieutenant Garret Purcell. The Irish had no artillery and could only blockade the castle which had some four hundred people within its walls. The castle surrendered due to lack of drinking water on 18th May that year and everyone was allowed to leave unharmed after Barbara Brown negotiated a ceasefire. It is said that Patrick Purcell himself, escorted Dame Barbara Brown as far as the outskirts of Cork city.

The castle itself must have been substantial to protect some four hundred people within its walls, as well as a good number of cattle and sheep. Little is known of the buildings within the walls. Substantial damage was done to the outer walls and barbican. The main hall must have been built mostly of timber as the estimate of restoration gives the price of £300 for timber. It is reputed that a large library of books was confiscated by the Irish officers. God only knows what happened to this fine collection!

Castletown Castle 2
Parish: Castletown
Townland: Coolbaun
Barony: Coonagh
OS Sheet 66 ref 824 479
3 kilometres south-southwest of Doon, close to the Tipperary border.

This castle was built by the O'Hurleys at the end of the fourteenth century. Castletown Castle is located a short distance to the west of the old church on the edge of a stream. It is also referred to as the Castle of Mac Brian Coonagh.

O'Donovan described it as a magnificent ruin consisting of a large keep with a high square tower at the east end. The tower was constructed of lime stone blocks and measured on the outside base 6 metres by 3.5 metres. A spiral stairway ran to the top. The round-headed doorway is on the east side. The original height of the tower was over 26 metres.

The keep or main house part of the castle on the inside is about 9.5 metres in breadth and its length was probably over 16 metres. The existing part of the north wall is over 16 metres high and over 2.5 metres in thickness.

This was the main castle of Mac Brian Coonagh. Later it passed into the hands of the Earl of Thomond.

See also Castle Cluggin.

Castletown Castle 3
Parish: Kilcornan
Townland: Unknown
Barony: Kenry
OS Sheet 64 ref 388 560
This castle was situated a little to the west of Pallaskenry.

A fortress was erected by Danes near Castletown in 1041. In 1164 another castle was built which soon fell into the hands of the O'Donovans. Later in its history it was part of the Desmond possessions and in the Elizabethan wars it was forfeited to Sir Hardress Waller whose descendants built the much later house called Castletown on the site.

The castle was captured from Hardress Waller by the

Confederate forces in 1642. Hardress made a claim to the Crown for the loss and damages to the goods that were in the castle, which included bed linen, tapestries, pots and pans. This request was rejected by the Crown.

Cleanlis Castle / Castle English
Parish: Killeedy
Townland: Unknown
Barony: Upper Connello / Glenquin
OS Sheet 72 in the area of 240 230 or a little to the north.

Lewis refers to a strong fortress whose owner enjoyed special privileges but does not elaborate on this enigmatic reference.

Claonglaise was a wooded area said to be a retreat of the Geraldines in the wars with Elizabeth. This name is anglicized as Cleanglass, which is the name of two townlands in the hills south of Glenquin. Perhaps Lewis was referring to Glenquin Castle and using the term Cleanlis as a general one for the area. This is unclear and we have no other reference to Castle English.

See also Glenquin Castle and Killeedy Castle.

Cloghacloka Castle
Parish: Unknown
Townland: Cloghacloka
There is no record of the exact location of this castle. OS Sheet 65 area of 536 503 1.5 kilometres east of Patrickswell.

Westropp didn't even mention it in his list of castles in County Limerick. In *The Book of Limerick* there is a reference that in 1336 the castle was in the possession of one called 'De Galfrid Coke', hence the name Clogh Coke. From his name it must be deduced that he was a Norman knight with Welsh family connections.

In 1500 the property belonged to a Donnagh O'Brien according to the Seancas Sil Bhriain.

Clogh Castle
Parish: Croagh
Townland: Clogh East
Barony: Lower Connello east
OS Sheet 64 ref 395 440
4.5 kilometres northeast from Rathkeale and about 1.5 kilometres south of Cappagh Castle.

In O'Donovan's day (1840) only the east wall was standing. The rest of the castle had fallen into ruins.

Cloughkeating Castle
Parish: Unknown
Townland: Cloghkeating
OS Sheet 65 ref area of 540 518
Close to R526 2.5 kilometres northeast of Patrickswell.

The exact site of this castle is not known. There is a reference indicating that a Richard Keating seems to have been in possession c. 1336. In 1586 the castle and lands were held by Mac Morietagh O'Brien but were granted to Sir E. Fyton of Tervoe the following year.

In 1611 Sir Walter Agard held the castle and lands but in 1669 they were transferred to David and Henry Bindon and remained in the possession of the Bindons until 1757.

Clonshire (Cloonsheer) Castle
Parish: Cloonsheer / Cluain Siar – western potato
Townland: Graigue or Clonshire Beg
Barony: Lower Connello east
OS Sheet 65 ref 424 447
Situated west of Adare.

This castle was about half of a mile southeast of the old church ruins. This was a four-storey tower house of approximately 9 metres by 7 metres. The ruins indicate that the lower vaulted chamber was blocked by the building of a spiral stairway to the upper rooms. This was probably a later modification when a new wing and entrance were added. This later part had a caphouse higher than the main tower. Another wing of three storeys was added at the other end at a later date.

Very close to Garraunaboy Castle.

Cluggin Castle (Castle Cluggin)
Parish: Castletown Coonagh / Tuoghcluggin / Tuath an Chluigin – district of the little bell
Townland: Castle Cluggin
Barony: Coonagh

OS Sheet 66 ref 805 435
3 kilometres northwest of Oola on the N24

The ancient site of this castle was in the townland of Cluggin or Castlecluggin. It is reputed to have been first the property of Mac Brien O'gCuanach and later the Earl of Thomond. It is mentioned in the MS. Pedigree of the O'Briens but it not shown on the latest ordinance survey maps.
  No history available.
  See also Castletown Castle 2.

Corgrig Castle
Parish: Unknown
Townland: Corgrig
Barony: Connello
OS Sheet 64 ref 256 511
Just south of Foynes, close to N69.

This castle was built by the Desmonds and is situated not far from Robertstown. Very little remains. It is recorded that it was blown up with gunpowder during the Elizabethan period.
  It is generally accepted that this was originally a Desmond castle. It was mentioned in an Inquisition of 1540 as being occupied by Don Gow, who was a constable of the Earl of Desmond. It is said that Don Gow levied a tax on the fishing boats that went up the river to Limerick, especially the oyster boats, on which he levied a hundred oysters from each boat. Foynes in those early days was just a fishing village. In 1587 after the failed Desmond Rebellion the castle and lands were forfeited and handed over to a William Tren-

chard when he paid £1,000 at a London auction of these Irish properties.

Trenchard was, in fact, granted some 14,000 acres on the condition that he should retain some 1,500 acres for his own use and employ English settlers on the remainder. These conditions were not fulfilled as he could not get English settlers to move to Ireland and as a result he had to take on Irish tenants, many of whom previously worked the lands prior to the Desmond Rebellion. After the death of the Earl of Desmond and the introduction of the Act of Pardon by Elizabeth, Thomas Cam Fitzgerald made a petition to Elizabeth that his lands, which had been granted to Trenchard, be restored to him. This was rejected.

William Trenchard was succeeded by his son Francis, who became known for evicting the native Irish from his land. He granted some lands to a Richard Gill and Emry Lee. Fearing for his own life he always kept a platoon of troops at the castle and they accompanied him whenever he left the castle to inspect his lands or travel elsewhere. Francis died in 1622 and the family continued to live in the castle until they moved into a Georgian mansion nearby which was called Mount Trenchard.

Sir George Carew, Lord President of Munster, laid siege to Corgrig Castle in 1600 when it was taken over by the Irish insurgents, just prior to the Battle of Kinsale. He took possession after a short siege and installed Oliver Stephenson. Stephenson was an Elizabethan undertaker who was given all the lands of the Wall family of Dunmoylan. Somehow, the Trenchards regained possession of the castle and lands and they leased them to Arthur and John Ormsby. Sometime later Stephen and W. Palmes took over the lease and by the end of the eighteenth century a Griffin family was in occupation of a new mansion built on the site of the old castle.

Corrin Castle
Parish: Killeely / Cill Fhiadhaile – church of St. Fiadhal
Townland: Coonagh West
Barony: Liberties of Limerick
OS Sheet 65 ref 535 580
Close to the north bank of the Shannon, west of Limerick city, close to an airfield.

The ruins of this castle are to be found in Coonagh West. When surveyed in 1840 there was very little remaining except a part of the west wall, which was 6 metres in height and less than 1 metre in thickness. It was impossible even at that time to judge the full original extent of this castle.

Courtbrown Castle
Parish: Askeaton
Townland: Courtbrown
Barony: Lower Connello east
OS Sheet 64 ref 340 540
3.5 kilometres due north of Askeaton, overlooking the Shannon estuary.
Mentioned in Lewis but nothing known.

Court Castle
Parish: Kildimo / Cill Dioma – church of St. Dima
Townland: Court
Barony: Kenry
OS Sheet 65 ref 475 526
Beside the river Maigue and close to the N69 2.5 kilometres east of Kildimo.

Nothing available as to its history. It possibly belonged to the Purcell family who had other holdings nearby.

Crecora Castle / Ballinveala Castle
Parish: Crecora / Craobh Comhratha – bush of the sign
Townland: Ballinaveala
Barony: Pubblebrien
OS Sheet 65 ref 530 459
4 kilometres south of Patrickswell and 2 kilometres south-west of Crecora village.

The castle is situated in the south of the townland of Ballinaveala. The ruins of the castle were still visible in 1840. It was situated on high ground and measured about 8.5 metres by 4.5 metres inside. The height was 16 metres at that time, amounting to 4 storeys.

On the west side and joined to this tower was a court. Some of the quoinstones were still visible on this west wall. No ruins remain of the court.

Creggane Castle
Parish: Colmanswell
Townland: Creggane
Barony: Connello Upper
OS Sheet 73 ref 533 258
2.75 kilometres north of Charleville, just west of the N20.

Mentioned in 1583 as a turreted tower with a bawn, by the mid-nineteenth century the tower had been lowered and roofed.

Croagh Castle
Parish: Croagh
Townland: Adamstown
Barony: Lower Connello East
OS Sheet 65 ref 408 428
6 kilometres northeast of Rathkeale in Croagh Village.

This castle was attached to the western end of the old parish church.

Croom Castle
Parish: Croom / Croma
Townland: Croom
Barony: Coshma
OS Sheet 65 ref 512 408

Croom contained an extensive round bawn with high turrets. Reputed to have been built on the bank of the Maigue River by Dermot O'Donovan during the reign of King John to protect the ford across the river. Dermot had at this time gained possession of the territory earlier ruled by the Mc'Eneirys (MacEnernys) who were the local Irish clan. When the O'Donovans were later driven out by the O'Briens c. 1200 and ended up in Kerry and West Cork, the castle was rebuilt by the Earl of Kildare making it his principal seat and taking from it the war cry of 'Crom-a-Boo'.

O'Donovan stated that when he visited the ruins c. 1840 he had great doubts as to whether any part of the ruins dated from the thirteenth century. There was one square tower remaining and this was only about four hundred years old. The O'Donovan clan probably had a residence here but the castle was built at a later date.

Croom and Adare were closely linked together. When Walter De Lacy died during the reign of Edward I, his possessions were divided amongst his two surviving sisters. Margaret, the eldest, married John de Verdon, was now in possession of part of the De Lacy's lordship of Meath and the office of Chief Constable of Ireland. On the other hand, the castles and manors of Adare and Croom passed to Maurice Fitzgerald, of the Kildare branch of the Geraldines. In 1310 the first Earl of Kildare obtained Royal permission to wall the town of Croom. It was regarded as the ancestral home of the Kildare Geraldines. On the outlawing of the Earl of Kildare in 1537, Croom was bestowed on the Earl of Desmond for life but early in the next century it reverted to its former owners.

During the reign of Elizabeth the castle was attacked by the English. The Geraldines were besieged on at least three occasions in the castle. Red Hugh O'Donnell rested here with his army on his way to Kinsale. Late in 1600, when the castle was attacked by Sir George Carew on his way to Glin Castle, most of the defending garrison under Pierce Lacy, who was the custodian, escaped during the night and the castle surrendered the following day.

In 1610, the Castle and Manor was restored to the Fitzgeralds by King James and, in the Insurrection of 1641, it was forfeited. Later, in 1678, it was granted to the Duke of Richmond by his father Charles II. The Duke resided in the castle for several years and later sold it to the Croker family.

In 1691 the castle was garrisoned by the troop of James II, but with the advance of King William, after the Battle of the Boyne, the garrison fled to the safety of Limerick. After this event, the castle passed back to John Croker who rebuilt it. The castle later passed into the hands of a Colonel Dickson, who later sold it to a Colonel Russell, brother of F.W. Russell, M.P.

After being unoccupied for generations Croom Castle was rebuilt as a residence in the early nineteenth century.

Some two miles away is Tory Hill where Sir James Fitzgerald, brother to the Earl of Desmond, fought the English forces under Elizabeth's commander, Malby. The Irish force of some two thousand men was defeated and some two hundred and fifty were killed. Amongst the fallen was Dr. Allen, the Roman legate at that time.

Note: It is said that the bards of Croom Castle first introduced the famous verses that we know today as 'Limericks'. In the middle of the eighteenth century, Croom became the meeting place of the Irish poets. Usually they met in the tavern belonging to Sean O'Tuama. It was like a continuation of the great bardic schools. They wrote elegies, love songs, drinking songs, songs of patriotism and verses, which became known as 'Limericks', later translated by James Clarence Mangan.

Cullam Castle

Parish: Kildimo / Cill Diama – church of St. Dima
Townland: Court
Barony: Kenry
OS Sheet 65 ref 475 520
700 metres south of Court Castle, 2 kilometres east of Kildimo old church.

Cullam Castle was situated on the lower reaches of the Maigue river on a hill overlooking Court Castle which was almost directly below it on the river's edge. According to tradition it was built by one of the Fitzgeralds in 1514.

In 1651 it was described as a fine strong castle and stronghold which was held by a sizeable Irish garrison under Thady Burke. When Sir Hardress Waller began his siege Burke refused to surrender the castle but when cannons began firing he was forced to conclude a surrender. The English marched into the bawn and within minutes they were fired upon by those on the battlements of the tower who had not been notified of the surrender. Two English soldiers were killed and Sir Hardress was wounded in the arm. Even though the English soldiers wanted revenge, Sir Hardress calmed his soldiers and an honourable surrender was agreed.

Little remains of this fine castle except a heap of rubble, as it was destroyed by gunpowder at some later stage.

Derreen Castle
Parish: Kilcornan
Townland: Derreen
Barony: Kenry
OS Sheet 65 ref 419 524
Close to the N 69 8 kilometres east of Askeaton.

Also called Castle Grey, this was a tower with a floor plan approximately 16 × 6 metres.

Derryknockane Castle
Parish: Unknown
Townland: Derryknockane
OS Sheet 65 ref in the area of 560 510
There is no record of the exact location of this castle, but it would have been roughly 4.5 kilometres northeast of Patrickswell.

It seems that it was originally a castle of the O'Briens who were trying to get a foothold in the area.

It is recorded that Lord Grey, in 1536, captured this castle from Teige Bacach and some other O'Briens. Somehow, the castle was restored to Teige after some money passed hands. It appears that one Stephen Sexton occupied the lower chamber in 1591 as a caretaker. A Dominic Roche was in possession in 1607. Sometime later in 1634 a Daniel O'Brien held the castle and at his death left it to a David Bourke. It was then in a fairly ruined condition.

Donaman (Dunnaman) Castle
Parish: Croom / Croma / Cromedh
Townland: Dunnaman / Dun na mBeann – fort of the gables
Barony: Coshma / Upper Connello / Pubblebrien
OS Sheet 65 ref 473 424
4 kilometres west-northwest of Croom

This castle is located a short distance west of Dysert round tower and ancient church. It was described as a low broad tower measuring some 15 metres by 10.5 metres and the walls were about 10 metres high, which was probably the original height. With the thickness of the walls being about 2.5 metres, the interior space was extremely limited. To the right of the entrance is a passage to the guardroom and on the roof of this passageway is a hole by which an enemy could be attacked from above. Passages and small chambers occupy the upper storey.

This castle seems to have been erected some time prior to 1506. It is stated in the *Annals of the Four Masters* that 'Catherine, the daughter of the Earl of Desmond, Lady of Hy-Carbery, had this castle built as well as "Beann-Dubh".' In early days this castle was called Beann-na-mBeann Castle. The castle is situated between Croom and Adare.

On the outer walls of the castle a 'Sheela-na-Gig' can be seen. Another one can be seen on the wall of the nearby castle of Tullovin.

Doon Castle
Parish: Doon / Dun – fort
Townland: Doon / Dun Bleisce – fort of Blesc
Barony: Owneybeg
OS Sheet 66 somewhere in the area of 835 510

The name derives from an ancient fort which was located in the townland.

This is Dun Bleisce, which takes its name from a famous harlot who lived in the area in earlier times. She is mentioned in many accounts by many of the ancient Irish writers so she must have been more than notorious in her day.

In 1829, Doon Castle was repaired by a Walter O'Grady, the then owner of the lands in the locality. He is reputed to have built a number of towers near the castle but no remains can be found today.

Doondonnell Castle
Parish: Doondonnell / Dun Domhnaill – fort of Donell
Townland: Cloghnarrold
Barony: Connello Lower
OS Sheet 64 ref 343 420
2.5 kilometres west of Rathkeale, close to the Holy well and ancient church site.

There were some ruins not far from the old church in Cloghnarrold townland in 1840. These old ruins indicated that a castle probably stood in this area sometime earlier.

There is no further information.

Drombanny Castle
Parish: Donoghmore / Domhnach Mor – great church (also called Cahirnarry parish)
Townland: Drombanny
Barony: Clanwilliam
OS Sheet 65 ref 609 519
Situated about 6 kilometres from Limerick city on a hill about 1.5 kilometres west-southwest from the old church ruins.

Only about 3 metres of the south wall remained in 1840. No other details were obtainable.

Dromore Castle
This is not an ancient castle, as it was built c. 1840, but it does deserve a passing mention.
It is a fairy-type castle like something out of Bavaria with

its towers and turrets which was built as a country residence by the third Earl of Limerick. The cost of building this castle almost bankrupted the Earl. The castle was only temporarily lived in as it suffered from severe dampness through its 2-metre thick limestone walls, which were almost porous. The castle was closed finally in 1915 and was sold in 1939 and bought by a Limerick merchant. The roof was removed in 1956. It is still one of the most interesting buildings in Ireland despite its state.

Drumkeen House
Parish: Drumkeen / Drom Caoin – peasant ridge
Townland: Drumkeen
Barony: Clanwilliam
OS Sheet 65 ref 726 474
1.5 kilometres southwest from Dromkeen Bridge (N24).

According to Fitzgerald in his *History of Limerick Vol. I* (p. 284) there were ruins of this building, which was called Drumkeen House. It is not known if this was a fortified mansion or some other type of building but since it was occupied by the Burkes and given the early dates it may have been a substantial mansion going back to the reign of Charles I. It is possible that this was the second house of the Burkes after Castle Troy.

The ruins were still visible in 1840 but no further information is available.

Dunmoylan Castle
Parish: Dunmoylan
Townland: Dunmoylan

Drombanny Castle

Barony: Lower Connello
OS Sheet 64 somewhere in the region of 272 443

There is a possible castle site here. O'Donovan stated that, according to local tradition, a few hundred metres south of the old church, a castle or court stood in olden days. Nobody local had any recollection of seeing any ruins or walls. Lewis referred to this as a doon or fort, implying that it was a pre-medieval fort where a castle was built within.

Dysert (Disert) Castle
Parish: in joint parishes of Robertstown and Shanagolden: Robertstown – town of Robert
Townland: Dysert
Barony: Lower Connello
OS Sheet 64 ref 286 506
Situated about 5.5 kilometres west of Askeaton close to Robertstown Creek.

The castle measured about 6.2 metres by 4 metres on the inside. The walls were about 16 metres high and about 1.5 metres in thickness. There were four storeys. One arch remained in 1840. This castle was never attacked by cannon fire but fell into ruins over the centuries. It was probably built by the Anglo-Norman Edmond Fitz Philips c. 1586 and was occupied by Edmond Fitz Philips who was in possession of the lands of the territory of Morgans, but these facts cannot be verified. The castle and lands remained in that family up to the Desmond Rebellion when Edmond was killed. During the period from 1628 to 1655 it was in the possession of Sir Richard Wingfield. The occupants over the

Dromore Castle

centuries seemed to have remained loyal to the Crown, regardless of what happening around them.

Esclon (Esclone) Castle
Parish: Kilkeedy
Townland: Unknown
Barony: Pubblebrien
OS Sheet 65 Area of 495 555

This castle was situated to the west of Mungret, near or on the site of Carrigogunnel. Both the castle and the name have now vanished. The manor of Esclon is now the area comprising the parish of Kilkeedy.

It seems that the original fortification was of Norse origin. It is not known if there was an earlier Irish fort in the location. Around 1200, Esclon was in the hands of William de Burgo, who was known by the Irish as William the Conqueror. He had married the daughter of Donald O'Brien, prince of Thomond, to consolidate his position around Limerick. When his son, Richard, died in 1213, the manor and lands reverted to King John of England. The castle was in ruins in 1499. Other sources say that the area known as Esclon was given by James Mac Garrott, Earl of Thomond to one Brian Dubh O'Brien, who was a descendant of Prince Teige Glemore O'Brien, who died in 1426. He was the son of Concubhar O'Brien who was the chief of Thomond from 1406 to 1414, and his wife Mary MacMahon of Clare. Brian Dubh had only one son called Donough but he had eleven sons who each, except one, received a portion of the land which by then became known as Pubblebrien.

Dysert Castle

The name (Aos Cluan) had disappeared from use and was superceded by the name 'Fossagh Lymerey', which means the bog or wastelands of Limerick, as this land was prone to flooding in bad weather. In time, the name was changed to Pubblebrien. By c. 1419 the church of Esclon had merged with the parish of Kilkeedy.

Fanningstown Castle
Parish: Fedamore / Faidh Damair – wood of Damar
Townland: Fanningstown
Barony: Small County
OS Sheet 65 ref 498 443
3.5 kilometres southeast of Adare.

This was a tower house, of which ruinous traces remained up to 1850. These consisted of pieces of walls about 2 metres high measuring about 18 metres by 9 metres, all of which have now completely disappeared. The castle was in the possession of the Fanning family until the late 1500s before the Earl of Desmond came into ownership. This castle is not to be mixed up with Fanning's Castle, also known as Whitamore Castle in old Limerick city.

Refer to Castle Roberts for additional information on the area.

Fantstown Castle
Parish: Kilbreedy Major / Cill Bhrighde – church of St. Bridget
Townland: Fantstown

Barony: Coshma
OS Sheet 73 ref 649 279
Situated a short distance to the right on the road from Kilmallock to Knocklong, about 3.75 kilometres east of Kilmallock.

The castle measured about 10 metres by 6.3 metres and the thickness of the walls was almost 2 metres. There is an arch on the ground floor. The staircase is spiral and runs to the top of the castle. The height was about 16 metres and there were three storeys. It seemed that there was an arch also on the second floor. In O'Donovan's opinion there were originally four floors and the castle was much higher, possibly over 20 metres. Some of the fireplaces were in reasonable condition. Three of the chimneys still remained. Near the top on the outside are two sentry boxes – one attached to the north wall and the other to the southeast wall.

Fedamore Castle

Parish: Fedamore
Townland: Castlequarter
Barony: Small County
OS Sheet 65 ref 598 438
1 kilometre east of Fedamore village and church and 2 kilometres west of the site of Skool Castle. Also only about 2.5 kilometres north of Glenogra Castle.

This castle or tower house was situated in the townland of Castlequarter but no remains exist today. The territory was originally the property of the Earl of Desmond but was later granted to the Earl of Thomond.

Finnitterstown Castle
Parish: Kilfenny
Townland: Finnitterstown / Baile anFhirteara / Baile Fiteera
Barony: Upper Connello
OS Sheet 65 ref 443 423
The site of this castle is about 3 kilometres east of Croagh.

According to O'Donovan some ruins could still be seen in 1840. These consisted of the east and south walls to a height of about 2 metres. Dimensions could not be taken. It is thought originally to have been a castle of four storeys with arches on the bottom two. Lewis states that it belonged to the Earls of Kildare.

Garraunboy Castle
Garranboy (Gurran Buidhe) Castle
Parish: Clounshire
Townland: Garraunboy
Barony: Lower Connello east
OS Sheet 65 ref 435 444
Possibly Garran Beg Castle
Located a few hundred metres from the old church of Cloonsheer, only about 1.5 kilometres from Clonshire Castle.

This castle was in total ruins in 1840 with only parts of the walls visible.

It had been a five-storey tower house measuring about 14 metres by 9 metres. The outer end wall has fallen but the remainder still stands in ruins. The fourth storey was vaulted. The tower was surrounded by a small rectangular bawn with four round corner turrets, which were all approx. 5 metres in diameter. One of these turrets had a vault and a number of gun loops.

Garryfine Castle
Parish: Bruree
Townland: Garryfine
Barony: Lower Connello
OS Sheet 73 in the area of ref 505 292
Situated about 4 kilometres southwest of Bruree.

This castle was held by Richard Mac Thomas Fitzgerald prior to the Geraldine Rebellion in 1583. Richard was killed and his lands were confiscated and handed over to George Bouchier after the Geraldine rebellion and sometime later Henry Oughtred held the lands of Garryfine and Cloinfearta, including the castles in the territory.

Glebe Castle
Parish: Rathkeale / Rath Gaela
Townland: Castlematrix
Barony: Connello Lower
OS Sheet 64 ref 357 412
This castle stood about 300 metres from Castlematrix Castle.

Like Rathnaseer, it was a small castle and much more like a watch tower. It measured about 7 metres by 4.2 metres and had three storeys. The existing walls were about 13 metres high in 1840 and about 2 metres thick. There were no arched floors and the castle was inhabited at that time.

Glenogra Castle
Parish: Cahircorney or Glenogra / Gleann Ogra – vally of Ogra (ancient chieftain)
Townland: Glenogra
Barony: Small County
OS Sheet 65 ref 592 418
By the R511, 15 kilometres south of Limerick, situated east of Rathmore on the banks of the Camoge River not far from some church ruins.

It was described as a strongly fortified enclosure (bawn) measuring about 50 metres long by 35.5 metres broad and the walls were over 8 metres high. The wall is built of limestone blocks and is very strong. At the northeast corner stands a massive octagonal tower which had a diameter of about 6.25 metres with a dome vault and stairway following the wall contours. It was four storeys high with walls which are 2 metres thick. There was a stonework arch on the second storey. On one side of the octagon rises a small square tower with an interior spiral stairway. On another tower that was very similar there was a tall chimney, which was higher than the main tower itself. This seemed to be a later addition. There are indications that there was some sort of projection between both towers.

At the north wall were four vaults over which a tower existed in earlier times. On the south side is the main entrance to the enclosure (bawn) where cattle were protected at night. Ruins of the tower on the south corner were in existence in

1840 but it is not known if the other three towers were actually completed. More than likely they were. A narrow wall replaced the original walls on the south and north and extended further by about 20 metres from the original enclosure, as if to indicate there were two other small enclosures. Lewis refers to its many cellars and underground stairways.

There is no definite date of building but it was probably originally a thirteenth-century structure of the Fitzharrises or the De Lacys. It subsequently belonged to the Earl of Desmond. O'Donovan stated that the octagonal tower was, in his opinion, from a later period. This could be true but why were the builders following the design of the Knights Templar? Even though I have great regard for O'Donovan and Curry as sources, maybe they were rushing and made wrong conclusions!

Refer to Rathmore.

Glenquin (Glinquin) Castle
Parish Killeedy / Kill-Ide – church of St. Ide
Townland: Glenquin
Barony: Upper Connello
OS Sheet 72 ref 247 263
This castle is situated about 2 kilometres to the west of the ruins of Kileedy Castle, beside the R515 at Glenquin Bridge.

This was a fine lofty castle of seven storeys and measuring at its base 10 by 12.5 metres approximately. It is related that in A.D. 1266 Mahon O'Cuilcin, Lord of Claonglaise, was stabbed to death by his own wife in a fit of jealousy in the bedchamber of this castle. According to tra-

Glenogra Castle

dition this castle was built by the O'Hallinans around 1462 but was soon seized by the O'Briens who held it until they were dispossessed by the O'Hanlons, who were in turn expelled by the Geraldines. In A.D. 1535 there was a battle somewhere near Glinquin where the Mac Auleys defeated and killed the Lord of Claonglais, who happened to be a Fitzgerald, as well as a relation of the Fitzgibbons. A large part of Fizgerald's army was made up of the gallowglasses called Mac Sheehy. These were also decimated. In the Desmond Rebellion the castle was captured by Captain Raleigh and in 1591 was granted to a Sir W. Courtney, together with Killeedy Castle. The castle was repaired by a Mr. Fulong, agent of the Earl of Devon, and continued in good condition down to modern times.

The Knights Templars built Temple Strand at Strand, 1.5 kilometres north of Glenquin, in 1291.

Glenstal Castle
Parish: Abington
Townland: Unknown, possibly Garranbane
Barony: Owneybeg
OS Sheet 65 area of 738 567

Prior to the Cromwellian confiscations, the O'Mulryans (Ryans) had a castle near the present Glenstal Abbey. It was taken over by the Stepneys, who built some terraced gardens near the castle. George Evan took over the castle, which he demolished and replaced with a new house in 1717. About a hundred years later, Sir Matthew Barrington took over the property and built a replica of a thirteenth-century castle, which later became the famous Abbey of Glenstal.

Kilmallock Castle

Lisamotta Castle

Glin Castle

Glin (Glynn) / Gleann Corbrai – glen of the Corbrai (ancient tribe)
Parish: Kilfergus / Cill Fearghasa – church of St. Fergus
Townland: Gleann Corbraighe / Cloch Gleanna
Barony: Shanid division of Connello
Referred to as 'Vallirupes' by Philip O'Sullivan Bere
OS Sheet 64 ref 131 475
Situated on the banks of the small Glencorbry River.

The remains of the original Glin Castle are situated on the edge of the town. The original massive square tower was built on a rock in the bed of the Glencorbally River, close to the Shannon, where it protected an ancient bridge.

The Irish Annaliste referred to the castle as 'Cloch Gleanna'. A sketch of about A.D. 1600 showed a rectangular walled bawn with a tower house in one corner and rectangular towers on the other three corners. What remains now is just the fairly damaged tower. The extensive ruins of the castle were still to be seen in 1866. They consisted at that time of two towers and another tower and banqueting hall, which were near the church. Most of the extensive vaults were to be seen, almost in perfect condition. The outer walls enclosing the bawn were 34 metres in length by 30 metres wide. The main entrance was to the north and was defended by a semi-circular rampart in front. Nothing much remained in 1896 except for the keep, which measured externally some 12 by 11 metres with walls 2.5 metres thick built of thin flagstones and cemented with lime and sand mortar. All that stood at that time was some 13 metres of the keep. On the east corner of the keep was a turret. According to the sketch in the *Pacata Hibernia*, the keep was situated in the southwest corner of the bawn, while there were two turrets defending the opposite wall. The castle enclosure was surrounded by a moat, which was fed by the Shannon River. A combination of the river in flood and high tide brought the water up to the very walls.

The Knights of Glin, who were a branch of the Geraldines, held the castle uninterrupted for some 600 years, except when it was forfeited for some time during the reign of Elizabeth and Henry VIII for a few years before being restored in 1602. The Knight of Glin was also known as the Black Knight.

Sometime in the middle of the fourteenth century the Fitzgeralds established themselves in Glin. They were first called the Knights of the Valley but this changed in later years to the Knights of Glin. As to how this title came into being is another question. It is said that when the Geraldines and their armies fought at the side of Edward III in Scotland that they were knighted on the battlefield for their valour. As they were dressed in different colours, the Green Knight became known as the Knight of Kerry; the Black Knight became the Knight of Glin, and the White Knight just retained that title.

The Knight of Glin was involved in the Rising of the Geraldines in the sixteenth century. The Knight and his son, Thomas, were captured and sentenced to death. The Knight successfully appealed this sentence using ancestors' participation in the war against the Scots and his loyalty to the Crown but his son was hanged and quartered at Limerick in 1567. His mother, who was present at the execution, is said to have picked up the head of her son and drank his blood and then gathered up the other pieces of his body and bound them in linen sheets. Then the procession headed off the long distance to Glin accompanied by over a hundred keening women who lamented his death in that special way. On 12th March 1580, at the height of a Geraldine revolt, the

English under Pelham surprised the Irish in Cloonlehard woods. Their location was betrayed by a deserter. Over four hundred were killed. The man who betrayed the location took a young girl hostage and, on returning the following day from searching for booty, the young girl killed her abductor with an axe.

It may be interesting to note that the siege of Glin Castle was something similar to that of Carrigafoyle, which is further to the west in Kerry. Carew is quoted in the *Pacata Hibernia* as to the arrangements and the siege itself. It states that, during the spring of 1600, the Lord President awaited supplies from England before he went to the west from Limerick. With news of their arrival under the command of a Captain Harvey, Sir George Carew with fifteen hundred men began their march. He was joined by the Earl of Thomond. As he marched inland to avoid the rivers Maigue and the Deel, he was followed by an Irish army of some three thousand men who kept shadowing the English force. Arriving at Glin on 5th July, Captain Harvey had already anchored a number of ships with some heavy guns. The guns were transferred ashore two days later. One was faulty but was repaired. Also, during these two days there was some parleying but without success. When the bombardment commenced the garrison directed all their fire on the cannon placements, killing many of the gunners. A breach was made in the outer wall and the English entered. After hand-to-hand fighting the garrison retreated to the keep, then after the large heavy door was burned down the English entered and hand-to-hand fighting continued up the spiral stairway to the roof and the battlements. All of the Irish garrison were killed, thrown off or jumped from the roof. During the siege, the Irish force under the Knight of Glin and others, who were only two miles away, did nothing. There was too much mutual distrust amongst the leaders so no decision to attack the English could be made.

Gormanstown Castle
Parish: Athneasy / Beul Athan na nDeisig – burial ground
Townland: Gormanstown
Barony: Coshlea
OS Sheet 65 ref 663 325
About 4.5 kilometres southeast of Bruff, close to the Morning Star river.

The castle was in ruins in 1840. Measuring, on the inside, 5.6 metres by 2.5 metres, it could be considered a small towerhouse. The walls were a little more than a metre thick. There were two opposite doors: one on the south and one on north walls. There were a number of crosses with circles and various other figures depicted on each side of the south door. An arch existed above the ground floor. The height inside was over 8 metres.

Gortadrumma Castle
Parish: Dunmoylan
Townland: Gortadrumma
Barony: Connello
OS Sheet 64 ref 435 223
5.5 kilometres southwest of Shanagolden.

In this townland were the remains of an old castle. Parts of the walls were still standing in 1840. Nearby is a holy well called Tobar Righ an Domhnaigh; literally, the well of the king of Sunday.

No further information is available.

Gurtnetubber (Gort-na-Tiobrad) Castle
Springfield Castle
Parish: Killaliathan / Killagholehans / Killaholahan / Cilleach O'Liathain – church of O'Liathain
Townland: Springfield: Gort Na Tiobraid – field of the spring
Barony: Upper Connello
OS Sheet 72 ref in the area of 350 225
Castle is located about 1.5 kilometres northeast of Broadford.

This was the seat of the Fitzgeralds, Lords of Conlish. It was incorporated into the demesne of Lord Muskerry at Springfield and was in a fairly good state of preservation in 1896. Called 'Ager Fontis' by Philip O'Sullivan in relation to the Epic March of O'Sullivan Bere, this was a four-storey tower house measuring about 12.5 metres by 8.2 metres. It is now roofless. The tower had four gables and two round bartizans at opposite corners. There is a pistol loop guarding the main doorway. It was four storeys high and the second floor was arched. The windows were all small and of cut limestone blocks.

Though forfeited during the reign of Elizabeth, it continued to be occupied by the Fitzgeralds of Clonlish, the descendants of Thomas Cam Fitzgerald, until 1688. Somehow they remained on as tenants of the Courtenays, paying rent for the lands which had been theirs for centuries.

The castle is mentioned in the *Four Masters* in 1579, with the march inland of Sir John of Desmond with an Irish force and some Spaniards after landing on the Dingle Peninsula. It is said that he rested at the castle for some time and somehow the English at Kilmallock got information of his presence. At that time the Lord Deputy, Sir William Drury, captains Bagnall and Malby with the Earl of Kildare were at Kilmallock. The English sent a force of about five hundred men to engage the Desmond contingent and walked into an ambush which few of the English survived. Sir William Drury died soon after of his wounds. Sometime later Malby wiped out the disgrace of the British forces when he defeated the Desmond forces at Monasternenagh. The papal legate Dr. Sounders fell mortally wounded in this encounter.

When Sir John Fitzgerald departed to France following the Treaty of Limerick in 1691, the castle was taken over by the FitzMaurices. Earlier, one David Fitzgerald had implicated Sir John in the 'Popish Plot', during the period 1679 to 1692, but he was cleared of any involvement. Nearby is the modern residence of Lord Muskerry. This was later passed to the Deane family (Lord Muskerry) through marriage.

Grange Castle
Parish: Tullabracky
Townland: Grange
Barony: Coshma
OS Sheet 65 ref 628 406
Just west of Lough Gur, 1 kilometre north of Holycross crossroads.

Greenaun Castle
Parish: Inch St. Lawrence / Inis San'Lebhras – island of St. Lawrence
Townland: Inch Saint Lawrence North
Barony: Clan William
OS Sheet 65 ref somewhere in the area of 657 496 but all traces have disappeared.

The castle was built on a small hill not far north from the old church. It is said that the castle belonged to the Nunan family. Fitzgerald refers to this castle as Grenane Castle while Curry and O'Donovan speak of another ruin called Sean Chuirt Castle, also the name of the hillock on which it was built. This castle was located in the centre of the townland of Knockroe Mason.

Nothing now remains of this old castle or mansion except a heap of rubble covered in grass and gorse. It is reputed that the castle was destroyed by an earthquake. This might seem far-fetched but that area of Limerick was prone to earthquakes in times past!

Hospital Castle or Manor House
(also called Kenmare Castle)
Parish: Hospital
Townland: Hospital / Oispideal
Barony: Small County
OS Sheet 65 ref 707 355

Hospital was associated with the Knights Templar. The ruins of an old church still stand in the village. Inside its chancel, by the altar, were the figures of two knights in grey marble. One of them was supposed to have been the founder, probably Geoffrey de Marisco. The Commandery of Knights Templar was founded by Geoffrey de Mariscis (de Marisco) about 1226 when he was Lord Justice of Ireland.

The original Templar buildings were located about 5 kilometres west of the village of Hospital on a green hill that was known as Cnoc Áine from the ancient Irish name for the sun goddess. These have now disappeared. Refer to Knockainy Castle for Áine, who became a fairy queen and a banshee in Irish folklore. The buildings were later transferred to the Knights Hospitallers of St. John of Jerusalem. Early references state that it was known as the 'House of Any' (Áine) or Knockainy. In the ancient ruined church there are a number of interesting tombs. One in particular has the effigies of a mailed knight and his lady, while the others have two mailed knights in high and low reliefs. This hospice of the Hospitallers had a preceptor, provost, chamberlain, cook, servants and workers. Anybody who was destitute and came to the door was offered food and lodgings. If they wished to stay on they were allowed two meals a day, provided they worked for their keep.

At the west side of the ruined church part of a square tower is incorporated into the church structure. Its east wall forms part of the church building.

Queen Elizabeth granted these lands to Sir Valentine Brown who built a castle on a site in what is now the village of Hospital. This structure was known as Kenmare Castle after the Brown family became Earls of Kenmare.

Sir John Brown, who came into the possession of Hospital and the adjoining lands, was created Knight of Hospital and became a Member of Parliament c. 1642 and soon afterwards became a captain in the army of Strafford. He was killed in a duel by a Mr. Christopher Barnwall. By the 1830s the castle had disappeared and a cottage stood on the site.

Killballyowen Castle
Parish: Knockaney
Townland: Killballyowen
Barony: Small County
OS Sheet 65 ref 658 370
Located about 3 kilometres east of Bruff.

By the 1830s, it had been incorporated into a dwelling house by DeCourcy O'Grady, who was known as O'Grady of Killballyowen. The O'Grady family also had a small castle in the village nearby.

It is reputed that the castle was built by the O'Grady family but nothing is known of its history.

Kilbehenny Castle / Kilcolman Castle
Parish: Kilbehany / Kilbeheeny / Glean nagCreabhar – glen of the Woodcock
Townland: Unknown
Barony: Coshlea
OS Sheet 74 area of 865 165

Situated a short distance northeast of the village of Kilbehenny. All that remains are some minor ruins of what was probably a small tower house.

This castle belonged to the family of the White Knight. It was here that he was held after being captured in one of the deep caves that are known today as Mitchelstown Caves. This was not the main cave but another smaller one, which was accessed by a long timber and rope ladder. After his location was betrayed, soldiers descended at night and apprehended him.

Edmund Spencer, the English poet and adventurer, spent some time in the castle. Cromwell took possession of Kilbehenny on 31st January 1649, and left a garrison there.

Kilcosgrave (Killcosgriff) Castle
Parish: Shanagolden / Sean-Ghualainn – old shoulder or hill
Townland: Kilcosgrave
Barony: Shanid Division of Connello
OS Sheet 64 ref 277 458
This castle was located about 3 kilometres southeast of Shanagolden.

There is very little information on this castle except that in 1840 there was a house in ruins built on the site of the old castle. This house was occupied by the Coplen family in or about 1677 and was later taken over by the Langfords through marriage. The family then became known as the Coplen Langfords. Castle was burned down in 1735.

Kilcullane (Kilkillaun) Castle
Parish: Kilkellane / Kilkillaun / Cill Chathlain – church of Cathlan
Townland: Kilcullane

Barony: Small County
OS Sheet 65 ref 672 397
The castle was situated about 2 kilometres southwest of Herbertstown.

This was a fifteenth-century castle of the Hurleys, situated on the west bank of the Camoge River and close to the remains of an early church.

This castle lay in ruins by 1840 when all that remained was the ground floor arch and portions of walls. The building measured about 7 metres by 4.5 metres with walls 2 metres thick. This was probably a small watchtower.

Kilduff Castle
Parish: Greane
Townland: Kilduff
Barony: Coonagh
OS Sheet 65 ref 776 459
Close to the N24 just to the southeast of Pallas Green New.

In the townland of Kilduff are the remains of a castellated house reputed to have been built by a branch of the O'Briens called the O'Briens of Coonagh.

By the mid-nineteenth century only parts of the west and south sides existed. Nothing remained of the other two walls. The existing walls measured about 12 metres by over 16 metres. The walls were 2 metres thick and had chimneys. The building was five storeys high. The windows indicate that it was built during the reign of James I.

Note: The barony map of 1657 shows this castle connected to Castletown Castle by a road.

Kilfinny (Killfenny) Castle

Parish: Killfeny / Cill Finnche – church of St. Finneach
Townland: Kilfinny
Barony: Upper Connello
OS Sheet 65 ref 462 398
Castle ruins are situated about 7 kilometres northeast of Ballingarry.

Built by Cormac MacEineiry in the reign of John it afterwards belonged to the Kildare family and has been described as a fine fortified mansion of the Elizabethan period. The walls were still standing in 1896. It consisted of two almost square towers. The south one measured 6 metres by 2.5 metres and contained two arched floors with two more storeys above. This tower was about 14 metres high with walls of over 1 metre thick. North of this building and joined to it was the main building which measured about 10 metres by 6 metres and had one arched floor with two more storeys over this. The walls were about 10 metres high and 1 metre thick.

Joining the north end of the main building was another tower that was similar to that at the south side. All the towers had pointed windows and loop holes. This was a very unusual building and has no equal in Ireland as far as we know. In a way it could be compared to Bunratty or Listowel but it is still different in construction. It seems that it was never subjected to cannon-fire.

It is said that this castle belonged to the Mac Eniry family, the ancient chiefs in the locality, whose principal castle was at Castletown.

This tower house is situated on a slope on the side of a high ridge. Within a 10-kilometre radius are the remains of some ten other castles. During the Insurrection of 1641 Kilfinny was defended by Elizabeth, wife of Sir John Dowdall, and daughter of Sir Thomas Southwell. Forming a small force of thirty horse and fifty footsoldiers from her retainers and tenants, she defended the castle for some ten months and even sallied out to attack the besieging force. She even went to the assistance of Croom Castle on five occasions. However, when a large cannon were brought to bombard the castle she yielded in order to avoid the loss of life. Patrick Purcell of Ballycullane was in charge of the besieging forces.

When the Irish forces took possession of Limerick Castle they also acquired a number of cannon. Now they had the means to attack the castles where the English had taken refuge. Amongst the cannons was a piece of some 404 kilo which could shoot a ball of 14.5 kilo. This was probably the biggest cannon in Ireland at that time and had been mounted on Limerick Castle walls for defensive purposes. The only problem was that it lacked a carriage. Improvising, a huge tree was hollowed out and the gun was placed inside. This was pulled by twenty-five yoke of oxen over bogs, marshes, streams and rough terrain. With the arrival of this monstrosity near their walls, castle after castle surrendered. Cappagh opened its gates, Castle Matrix was yielded up, Askeaton surrendered and Kilfinny hung out a white flag after receiving four direct hits from the great cannon on 29th July 1642. The long siege was conducted by Edy De Lacy before the arrival of the cannon.

Kilfinane Castle
Parish: Kilfinane
Townland: Kilfinane?
Barony: Costlea
OS Sheet 73 ref 682 232

It is said that an old castle of the Roches was situated in the town of Kilfinane.

Killanahan Castle
Parish: Killonahan
Townland: Killanahan
Barony: Pubblebrien
Also called Killelonehan
OS Sheet 65 ref 530 459
The castle was situated about 6 kilometres northeast of Croom.

This was a fifteenth-century castle built by Dermot O'Hurley.

Killeedy Castle
Parish: Killeedy / Kill-Ide – church of St. Ide
Townland: Killeedy North
Barony: Upper Connello
Killeedy: Church of St. Mida / Ita
OS Sheet 72 ref 270 263
Situated 2 kilometres east of Glenquin Castle, on a minor road 1 kilometre north of Ballagh.

The area is called after the ancient church of St. Ita founded in the sixth century. It is reputed that Saint Brendan, the navigator, in his younger days was educated here. The church was plundered by the Vikings in 838 and again in 851.

The castle was situated to the northwest of the old church on a small hill. Only a part of the south wall remained in

1840. It is reputed to have been built by King John or during the period of his reign. Other sources say it was a Templar castle. The Templars built Temple Strand at Strand, 1.5 kilometres north of Glenquin, in 1291.

Kilmacow Castle
Parish: Ballingarry
Townland: Kilmacow
Barony: Connello
OS Sheet 65 ref 455 376
Ruins of this castle were situated about 4.5 kilometres northeast of Ballingarry.

All that was mentioned in 1840 was that there were the ruins of an old castle or castle-like house in this townland. In the same townland is the high hill of Cnoc-Fir-inne where the legendary fairy king called Doon-Firinne was said to exist. Many tales were told in ancient days of people seeing him gathering his war-like troops on the side of the hill. It is said that this Doon or Dessa was the son of Milesius, the chief of the Milesians, who were one of the first groups of invaders to Irish shores.

Kilmallock Castle
Parish: Kilmallock
Townland: Unknown
OS Sheet 73 ref 608 277

Kilmallock seems to be called after 'Cill Mocheallog' – the church of Mocheallog (a seventh-century saint). Earliest references to Kilmallock, in the later half of the thirteenth century describe it as a walled town with four gates. The strong walls of the town made an oblong and at each angle there had been a castle, tower or fortification, one of which was the gaol of the town. There were four gates into the walled town. The castle or citadel, was situated in the centre of the settlement, and referred to as John's Castle. The building was rectangular and the height was about 20 metres with battlements on the top. Access was through the lower floor beside the guardroom. There were seventy-three steps in the spiral stairways to the top. One of the gates which still exists was called Blossom Gate.

Kilmallock was the principal town of the Desmonds and connected to that part of the family who were called the White Knights. The town later became an English settlers' enclave. Edward III granted the right of tolls and customs so that the walls could be kept in good order. Elizabeth granted another charter in 1584 while James I elevated the town to a borough in 1609.

Following the arrival of the Anglo-Normans, the Geraldines made themselves masters of the Golden Vein (Vale) with the town of Kilmallock as the centre of their power, as it commanded the road from Cork to Limerick.

The history of the town is, therefore, linked to the fate of the Desmonds. When the fifteenth Earl, called Gerald, was summoned to appear before the Lord Deputy he replied that he would return the following summer with 5,000 men to answer any allegations against him. He was immediately arrested and sent to the Tower of London where he was imprisoned for four years.

The leadership of the Desmonds passed over to James Fitzmaurice (MacMaurice), his cousin, who immediately attacked Kilmallock when the Lord Deputy departed. He was aided by the gallowglasses of Clan Sweeney and Clan Sheehy, who had come from Scotland. James totally destroyed the walled town on 2nd March 1571 and almost burned it to the ground. He was later captured and had to swear allegiance to the Crown on bended knees. Soon he was off to Europe seeking aid from the various monarchs and returned with a small force supplied by the Pope in 1579.

He was killed in a skirmish at Ballyvorheen in East Limerick shortly afterwards. His body was taken to Kilmallock and quartered above its gates and this was followed by the hanging of Patrick O'Hely, Bishop of Mayo, and a Franciscan friar, Father Con O'Rourke. Later, on his release from the Tower of London, Gerald had to give his young son, James, as hostage. Despite this fact, he continued fighting against the English and was killed in Kerry in 1582. This was the end of the house of Desmond except for some minor skirmishes. All the lands of the Desmonds were forfeited to the Crown.

When O'Neill and O'Donnell rose in the north they knew that they had to rally the forces of Munster. O'Neill came south and formally proclaimed that James Fitzgerald, nephew of the late Earl, was nominated the new leader of the Geraldines at Rath na Saor Castle near Ballingarry. James became known as the 'Sugan Earl' (the hay-rope Earl) amongst his enemies. With his influence growing in Munster the English got worried and released James, the son of the late Earl of Desmond, from his imprisonment in the Tower of London and proclaimed him Earl of Desmond.

Arriving at Kilmallock he received a tumultuous reception from the inhabitants but when he began walking towards the Protestant church of SS Peter and Paul the following morning everyone tried to dissuade him from going. When he came out of the church he was abused and spat on. After this showing of contempt he was of no further use to the Crown and was transferred back to the Tower of London where he died soon afterwards. He was soon followed to the Tower by the Sugan Earl, who had been betrayed for a thousand pounds by his relation, Edmond Fitzgibbon, the last White Knight. He also died in the tower in 1608. His body was later interred in the Dominican priory. A recumbent stone, now broken in two, marks his grave.

Kilpeacon Castle
Parish: Kilpeacon / Cill Beachain – church of St. Beacan
Townland: Kilpeacon
Barony: Small County
OS Sheet 65 ref 561 473
Ruins of the castle were situated 4.5 kilometres southeast of Patrickswell.

The original site of this castle was between the church and Kilpeacon House. In the reign of James I, this manor was granted to William King, Esquire, who built a very strong castle. The ruins of the old church have vanished off the landscape. Fitzgerald, in his *History of Limerick* mentioned 'a fine church with a handsome tower house' and that 'a castle stood near the church.' The castle was pulled down in the early nineteenth century, probably by a William King who built a fine mansion nearby. This building was in turn replaced by another mansion built by Edward Villiers.

A golden crown was found near the site of the old castle. This was later sold in Dublin by Mr. Villiers.

Knockainy Castle
Parish: Knockainy / Cnoc Áine – Áine's hill
Townland: Unknown
Barony: Small County
OS Sheet 65 ref 682 358
The ruins are located about 5.5 kilometres east of Bruff, close to Lough Gur and are to be found on the south side of the road between Hospital and Bruff and on the south side of the Hill of Áine on the western bank of river Comogue.

It measured about 7 metres by 4.5 metres. By 1840 there were only three floors visible with the bottom one arched. The height then was about 13 metres and the thickness of the wall was 2 metres.

A spacious and very strong fortress was erected here in about 1248 by John Fitzgerald (John of Callan). The castle is alternatively reputed to have been built by a Mathew O'Grady, who was steward to the Earl of Desmond. Other sources say that it was built by a Hogan and the last to occupy was a Hurley family.

The Geraldines and the Earls held court at the castle down to the middle of the sixteenth century. The O'Gradys looked after the castle and lands for the various earls. Their chief, in 1309, was killed in battle. After the fall of the Geraldines the lands of the O'Gradys were granted to Sir Thomas Standish. One of the O'Gradys married a daughter of Sir Thomas and, as a result, most of the O'Grady lands were restored.

Note: In the fourteenth century the Fitzgeralds erected two strong castles on the shores of Lough Gur, Doon and Black castles. See individual entries.

Knockatancashlane Castle
Parish: Cahirconlish
Townland: Knockatancashlane
Barony: Clanwilliam
OS Sheet 65 ref 682 502
Situated about 1 kilometre north of Caherconlish.

There is nothing definite known about this castle. It might have been built on the old fortress, which was known as 'cnoc-a-senachuis-leann'.
  See also Carrigarreely in this context.

Knocklong Castle
Parish: Knocklong / Cnoc Luinge – hill of the Camp
Townland: Knocklong East
Barony: Coshlea
Ancient name for Knocklong was Damh Goire
OS Sheet 65 ref 724 309
Castle was situated on a hill, 1 kilometre south of Knocklong town.

It is said that the hill got its name from when Cormac, King of Ireland, pitched his camp here when he was invading Munster. The castle stood on a high hill. It was in almost total ruins in the mid-nineteenth century. This was the seat of the O'Hurleys and could have been described as a strong tower house. When visited for the ordnance survey it was found that the quoinstones, the frames of the doors, windows etc., had been removed. It was not a high structure, maybe three or four storeys, measuring 6.5 metres by 5.75 metres on the inside. The walls were about 2 metres thick. There remained two apartments visible on the north wall and these had a number of large windows which had been vandalized. The castle was almost square, with four gables. From one of the gables protruded a plain chimney. The interior had been arched but the arch had fallen. The stone steps of the stairway had been removed. The castle is reputed to have been built in the middle of the fourteenth century.

This O'Hurley castle along with their lands was confiscated during the Cromwellian confiscations. Afterwards most of the O'Hurleys moved southeast into middle and West Cork.

See Ballinacarriga Castle in *The Castles and Fortified Houses of West Cork*.

Leagaun/Liagan (Tobernea) Castle
Parish: Effin / Eifinn / Cill Eifinn – church of St. Eifin
Townland: Leagaun
Barony: Coshma
OS Sheet 73 in the area of ref 602 237
This castle was located about 4 kilometres south of Kilmallock.

All that remains of this castle is a pile of stone and rubble.
No further details or history available.

Lickadoon (Lickadoen) Castle
Parish: Cahirnarry
Townland: Lickadoon
Barony: Clanwilliam
OS Sheet 65 ref 602 507
The ruins of this castle are situated about 8 kilometres southeast of Limerick.

In 1840 this was described as a very strong castle situated on a level section of land. This was a castle of two towers. At the eastern end it had a square tower which incorporated a spiral stairway to the top. The measurements of this section was 5 metres by 2.25 metres the inside. The main part of the castle on the western side measured over 7 metres by 5.3 metres on the inside. This part of the castle had five floors. Only the first and second remained in 1840, the upper floors having been destroyed. The walls had been over 22 metres high and almost 3.5 metres thick. Only a small part of tower ruins and a piece of wall remain today.

The castle originally belonged to the Hurley family and was later occupied by the Roches. It is said that the great archbishop of Cashel, Dermot O'Hurley c. 1530–1584 was born here. He was arrested after his arrival from Rome and charged with treason. When he denied the charges, he was tortured by roasting his legs in metal boots filled with boiling oil. He was then condemned to death and hanged in Dublin in 1587.

Limerick City

At one time, Limerick City had a number of tower houses and fortified dwellings and the view on approaching the city of these buildings and the strong walls with their fortified gate houses resulted in the description 'Limerick of the Castles'.

John's Castle
Situated on the King's Island, Limerick
OS Sheet 65 ref 578 578

This castle presents one of the best examples of Norman architecture in Ireland. The first castle building on the site took place c. 1200 during the reign of King John of England as a defence against the O'Briens and Thomond. Some sources say that it was built as early as 1185. There were references to its bawn c. 1200. It is said that the castle was built without a keep but recent excavations have revealed the base of a structure which could have been described as a banqueting hall. The castle or fortification was built roughly in the shape of a rectangle, with five sides with towers on each corner, and the Shannon River skirting one wall.

Initially it was fortified by four large circular towers. One of these was replaced by a bastion in 1611. Also, the towers were lowered and fortified by vaulting to support heavy guns. The entrance, which is situated on the north side, is flanked by two towers. There are indications that it had a portcullis above it. The bottoms of the walls were slanted outwards so that anything dropped from the battlements would bounce outwards towards an enemy. The round tow-

King John's Castle, Limerick

ers jutted out from the main walls so that archers could attack anyone trying to undermine the walls. In the inner bawn were located a great hall, accommodation and stables. The castle was surrounded by a moat fed by water from the river Shannon. Two D shaped towers flanked the main gatehouse which was located on the northwest wall. A long slit of a murder-hole protected the entrance between the towers which each had timber false floors to enable guns and ammunition to be passed up to the battlements. These towers were probably built in the latter half of the thirteenth century while the northwest tower is the oldest of the other towers.

The troops of the Earl of Desmond stormed the castle in 1332 but were driven out by the Crown forces shortly afterwards. It was again taken by the O'Briens and the Mac Namaras in 1369 and held by them for a short period.

The castle remained in disrepair until 1600 when Sir George Carew ordered that it should be restored and strengthened. This work was carried out by Sir Josias Bodley. The castle was forced to surrender during the Rising of 1642 to the Irish forces under Lord Muskerry after a short siege. In 1651 the Confederate forces holding the castle were forced to surrender after a protracted bombardment by the English forces under Ireton. During the war between King William and James, the castle was held by the Jacobean forces.

In 1691 the castle was besieged by the Williamite forces and in 1692 Patrick Sarsfield surrendered the castle under terms to Ginkle. This became known as the Treaty of Limerick, which was broken by the English 'before the ink was dry'. The castle was used as an English military barrack during the eighteenth and nineteenth centuries.

Tomcore Castle

This was a late-fourteenth century building in Irish Town at the junction of Mungret Street and John Street. A.T. Balbeyn called 'Cor' left the castle he had built to Limerick Corporation, should his brother from Bristol not wish to move to live in Limerick. In 1696 a market house was built on the site.

Galwey's Castle
Also known as Burke's Tower House
The remains are at Athlunkard Street, near the Cathedral.

A town Tower House or fortified medieval residence of the Burke family, probably built in the seventeenth century. John De Burgo of Galway was knighted by the Duke of Clarence for his defence of Baals Bridge against the O'Briens in 1361. The house was largely demolished in 1894 with the remains incorporated into a subsequent building. The 'V' shaped corbels which supported the floor beams can still be seen high up on the façade. Pieces of the original stone can be seen resting on the corbels and some recesses can be viewed. Vaulted cellars have been discovered together with old broken wine bottles.

Whitamore's Castle / Fanning's Castle
The remains of this castle or tower house are situated in the grounds of the Art College, in the centre of Mary Street, Limerick, opposite the old city jail.

Even though it was supposed to be a fortified house the windows are extremely large. Another section was built on at some later stage.

It was built by a merchant named Fanning, during the latter half of the sixteenth century or the beginning of the seventeenth, as his own private abode. He was executed by the

Cromwellian forces for his part in the defence of the city in 1651. Sometime later it became the property of Francis Whitamore, who was also Mayor of Limerick in 1681. Also sometimes referred to as Sarsfield's Castle or the Castle of Limerick. Sarsfield was reputed to have stayed here during the siege.

Shambles Castle
This house in High Street was made into a citadel in 1657.

Mr. Ffilkins Castle
Ffilkins Castle was near St Mary's church in the High Street.

Stritches Castle
A garrison or citadel in St Munchion's Parish.

Curragowre Castle
There seems to be little known of this structure other than that it was close to a weir on the Shannon.

The City Gates
There were seventeen gates into the city of Limerick, five for Irishtown and eleven on King's Island. Most of these were incorporated into the fortifications to facilitate existing routes, either to the bridge and County Clare or east to the friaries and the river, or to the Shannon quays.

East Watergate
Gets it name from Baal's bridge, which connected Irishtown with King's Island. This was an important city gate which guarded the approaches.

Watergate was probably the strongest and most important of the city gates.

St John's Gate
A map of 1580 shows a two-storey tower with two stepped gables sitting atop this gateway.

Mungret Gate, West Watergate, Thomond Gate, Island Gate, Sallyport, Little Island Gate, Abbeygate North, Fish Gate, Creagh Gate, Quay Lane Gate, New Gate and Castle Barrack Gate, would all have been fortified and defensible. The walls also had a number of towers as part of the fortifications. These included Cogan's Tower, Devil's Tower and Cromwell's Tower.

Lissamota Castle
Parish: Ballingarry
Townland: Lissamota
Barony: Upper Connello
OS Sheet 65 ref 418 387
This castle was situated approximately 3 kilometres north of Ballingarry.

See Woodstock Castle.

Lismakeery Castle
Parish: Lismakeery
Townland: Lismakeery
Barony: Lower Connello
OS Sheet 64 ref 326 475
2.5 kilometres south of Askeaton.

The ruins of this castle stand in farmland about 500 metres west of those of the fifteenth-century parish church.

It was a DeLacey castle and was occupied by that family until the time of Cromwell. Milltown Castle is close by.

Lisnacullia (Lisnacullin) Castle
Lisnacille Castle / Woodfort Castle
Parish: Loonagh
Townland: Lisnacullia / Lis Cluanin Each – fort of the meadows of horses
Barony: Lower Connello East
OS Sheet 64 ref 321 423
The substantial ruins of this castle are situated at the end of a private drive about 4 kilometres west of Rathkeale.

The castle was a rectangular tower house, three storeys high, which had a square wing or addition incorporated on the east angle with a spiral stairway running to the top. This addition had small rooms. The spiral stairway was difficult to ascend due to its structure and was lighted by loopholes at good intervals. Sometime later, another stairway was constructed over an arch at one of the angles of the building. The first floor was destroyed but the second, some 5 metres above, was in reasonable condition in 1840.

The next room above measured about 11 by 7 metres with three windows. Adjoining this, in the square tower is a small room measuring about 4 metres by 2.5 metres. Some vestiges of a polygonal bawn can still be seen measuring about 30 metres by 23 metres where there is an outbuilding or the remains of a small square tower or turret. Only two storeys remain:

This castle is reputed to have been built in about 1445 by the MacSheehys, who were brought from the Northwest of Scotland to fight as Gallowglasses (mercenary trained soldiers) by James Fitzgerald, seventh Earl of Desmond, c. 1420. The castle was on the site of the ancient 'Fort of the Wood' near Riddlestown Park.

The castle was confiscated after the Desmond Rebellion in 1579 and handed over to a Thomas Caune. It later fell into the possession of Donagh O'Brien in 1620 and in 1655 was held by Sir Edward Fitzgerald.

Longford Castle / Ballyneety Castle

Parish: Oolla Ulla – apples
Townland: Longford
Barony: Coonagh
OS Sheet 66 ref 845 445
The castle is situated right on the county border with Tipperary about 2.5 kilometres north of Oola Castle.

It is said that in 1691, General Sarsfield, having surprised the castle, blew it up after destroying the cannon and ammunition of William III, destined for the siege of Limerick. It is further reputed that it was later partially rebuilt, but sources disagree. This castle was in ruins in 1840 with only about 6 metres of the walls remaining. It was almost identical to the castle in Oola, measuring about 6 metres square and about 20 metres in height with five storeys containing very small chambers.

Lissamota Castle

Loghill (Loughill) Castle
Parish: Loughill
Townland: unknown
Barony: Lower Connello
OS Sheet 64 ref near 195 496
This castle was supposed to be located close to the N 69 Limerick to Tarbert road, between Foynes and Glin.

It was described as a strong castle or fortified house and was the property of the Bishop of Limerick. It was dismantled in the early nineteenth century and the stones used to build an estate wall.

Lower Shanid Castle
Parish: Kilmoylan
Townland: Shanid Lower
Barony: lower Connello
OS Sheet 64 ref 243 454
References indicate that this castle was situated about 3 kilometres south-southwest of Shanagolden.

This castle was supposed to be situated only a few hundred metres directly north of Shanid Castle itself. It is said that this was a much larger castle than Shanid and was the dwelling place of those who possessed the territory. Both castles were nearly always the property of the Earl of Desmond.

There are no remains except for a heap of stones.
See also Shanid Castle.

Pallaskenry Castle

Shanid Castle

Luddenmore Castle
Parish: Ludden / Ludden Beg / Luidin
Townland: Ludden Beg
Barony: Clan-William
OS Sheet 65 ref 642 479
The castle is situated about 1.5 kilometres south of the village of Inch Saint Lawrence on the north slopes of the hill called Boughhilbreaga, which is just west of the higher Knockroe.

According to Fitzgerald a strong castle stood at the foot of the hill called Knockroe. He refers to the castle of Ballybricken in this context but said no more. Ballybricken is actually further south but could also be said to be at the foot of Knockroe. Around 1600 a James Gould lived in Luddenmore Castle. It was forfeited in the Inquisition of Limerick in August 1623. Colonel Ingoldsby seems to have been granted this castle, as well as Ballybricken and the surrounding lands.

Maidstown (Baile Ui Bhenog) Castle
Parish: Drummin / Dromain-I-Chleircin – hill of the O'Cleircin
Townland: Maidstown / Baile Ui Bhenog – town of the young woman?
Barony: Coshma
OS Sheet 65 ref 585 319
The ruins of this castle are situated about 3.5 kilometres northeast of Bruree.

The castle is almost square measuring 11.25 metres by 10.3 metres on the outside. The walls were about 16 metres high and 1 metre in thickness. Adjoining is a building containing three storeys, which also contains the staircase. This part was originally of five storeys and O'Donovan stated that it was probably a later addition.

Maidstown was probably built by the O'Hanlons in the fifteenth century. Cromwell ordered it destroyed in 1654 but it survived almost entirely into the nineteenth century when part was occupied as a farmhouse. It was the birthplace of Daniel Webb, author of *Harmonies of Poetry and Music*.

Millmount Castle
Parish: Ballingaddy / Baile an Ghadaidhe – town of the thief (Ardpatrick)
Townland: Millmount
Barony: Coshma
OS Sheet 73 ref 615 275
This castle was supposed to be situated in the southeast of Kilmallock town.

According to Curry the remains of a castle were found in the northwest of the townland of Millmount. No idea of size or what actually remained was given.

Milltown Castle
Parish: Lismakeery
Townland: Milltown North
Barony: Lower Connello

OS Sheet 64 ref 342 472
3 kilometres south of Askeaton, on the west bank of the river Deel.

Like the nearby Lismakery Castle, this was probably a property of the De Lacys. Westropp in 1906, however, describes the site as a 'doubtful' castle, there being a fragment of an old house with a tall chimney in a ring wall.

Morgans Castle
Parish: Morgans / Muirgeadain
Townland: Unknown
Barony: Shanid Division of Connello
OS Sheet 64 ref in the area of 305 515
Situated about 3.5 kilometres west of Askeaton.

The Irish name for this parish signifies a maritime position. There is a vague reference to an early castle at Morgans which cannot be verified.

There are, however, some ruins located near Morgans House. It is possible that the remains were those of a manor house previously built by the Rose family which had fallen into ruins. However, the territory was in the possession of a descendant of the Fitzgeralds who had it for some seventy years. Earlier Morgans was held by John Fitzjohn, an ancestor of the Knight of Glin, and was part of the Manor of Shanid. In 1302 Morgans was referred to as Disert Marduin or Disert Mairgeoin.

Mungret Castle

Parish: Mungret / Mungairit / Mong Gairid?
Townland: Mungret
Barony: Pubblebrien
Imugram is also an old name for Mungret
OS Sheet 65 Area of ref 533 557
Located about 4.5 kilometres west of Limerick, north of the N69 close to Skehacreggaun.

The Knights Templars, otherwise known as the soldier monks, occupied the old Castle. They were renowned for their piety and their warlike spirit and they occasionally did defensive duty as custodians of nearby Carrig-o-Gunnell and were bound to render military service when called upon. It is reputed that a subterranean passage connected the house of the Knights Templars, which was a preceptory, referred to as Temple Mungret, with Carrig-o-Gunnell Castle. Local farmers have related that in certain places, if the ground is thumped with a sledge, there is a hollow sound along a line between the castles. Nobody has ever carried out an archaeological dig as the distance between the castles is over 3.5 kilometres and scholars say that the claim is nothing but folklore!

The Bindon family lived at Temple Mungret after being granted a large tract of land in the reign of Charles II (1665–1685). According to the Civil Survey of 1654, Temple Mungret then consisted of one plowland with a thatched house, fifteen cabins, four ruined churches and many stone walls. The castle of Mungret was in a fairly good state up to 1860. In that year it lost some 3 or 4 metres of its original height. The new owner of the land, who succeeded the Protestant bishop, had intentions of converting the castle into a mansion house. Thirty years later in 1890 the castle had completely vanished from the landscape.

There was a famous story where the Templars of Mungret, dressed as women, went washing clothes in the river near a ford where they knew that some other monks from Clonmacnois, who had questioned their knowledge of the Scriptures, were about to cross and visit them. They engaged their visiting co-religious in conversation in fluent Greek and Latin and the visiting monks halted their journey and turned back saying 'if the women of this area can speak different languages like that, we have no cause to be here'. It is said that many of the learned monks from the other Irish monasteries often came to visit and to listen to the 'learned women' after that encounter.

Newcastle (West) Castle 1
Parish: Newcastle
Townland: Newcastle
Barony: Upper Connello
OS Sheet 64 ref 279 337

Newcastle was called Castle Roe or Castle Nua O'Connaill earlier. This castle became the chief manor of the Geraldines in Munster.

The vaulted lower storey was still perfect in 1896. The walls which supported the arch were from 2.5 to 3.5 metres thick. The main building was described as being fitted up like a modern residence in 1896. Attached was a round tower for defence and a few metres away stood a square tower in good condition. On the other side stood the church and, from here, walls and underground passages ran down to the river. These were probably means of escape if required.

A short distance away is a large building, measuring 18 metres by 5.25 metres, which in later years became known as the Desmond Hall, probably a banqueting chamber. It had a fine vaulted ceiling and a black marble fireplace dating to c. 1638. Nearby is the Great Hall measuring 26 by 12 metres, approximately, which has some fine windows. The remaining parts of the castle are separated from the Great Hall by a modern wall. The keep and the peel house have been mostly incorporated into a modern building. Part of the south curtain wall, about 27 metres long and about 1.75 metres thick, joins the rounded flanking tower with the main keep, which is also round.

The castle is reputed to have been built by the Knights Templars c. 1184, some twelve years after the arrival of King John in Ireland. About 1332 on the instigation of the Church of Rome and the local bishops, the common people rose up against the Templars and killed many of them, by burning them at the stake, due to their so-called 'evil reputation and devil worship'. The castle reverted to the Crown and later became the property of the Geraldines. It is noted for its 'great Desmond Hall' where lavish gatherings were held.

The acorn and oak-leaf symbols of the Templars may be seen cut in a number of stones within the remains of the castle. Like all castles built by the Templars it was meant to last. It is reputed that Thomas 'an Apa' Fitzgerald extended the castle and built a circular bawn, parts of which can still be seen. He died in the castle in 1298 after serving as Justiciar of Ireland for a number of years. Two other earls died in the castle – Garrett (Gearoid Iarla), the fourth Earl, in 1399, and James, the eighth Earl, in 1598 – after the defeat of the Munster Geraldines.

It is not known when the descendants of Maurice Fitzgerald took over the castle. It is stated in O'Clery's *Book of Pedigrees* that the castle was in the possession of the family of the Earls of Desmond long before the title was created. Thomas Fitzgerald, grandson of John Fitzgerald who fell in the Battle of Callan in A.D. 1261, with his son, died at Newcastle after being in possession for some thirty years. Thomas was an infant when both his father and grandfather died.

O'Daly in his *History of the Geraldines* tells an interesting story which is abbreviated as follows – that the infant Thomas was in Tralee Castle when his nurse, on hearing of the deaths of his father and grandfather, ran about in a panic leaving the cradle unattended. An ape that was kept as amusement lifted the infant out of the cradle and carried him to the top of the castle in Tralee. It is said that the ape took off the swaddling cloths, licked him clean, dressed him again and brought him back down to his cradle. When the nurse entered the room, the ape hit her and screeched as if in reproach. After that incident the baby was called 'Thomas-an-appagh'. This tale is supposed to verify the ape in the arms of the Dukes of Leinster, which were the other family of the Geraldines, but they were not descended from Thomas Fitzmaurice. Thomas was the father of Maurice, the first Earl of Desmond, which title was created in 1329.

When Thomas was requested to look after his grandfather's second wife, Honora, daughter of the O'Connor, and her children, he granted her the lands and castles of Meine and Mahoonagh. This transfer was really made to Honora's eldest son called Gilbert or Gobbon. Hereafter that family was called Fitzgibbon or MacGibbon. Gilbert's eldest son, Maurice, was knighted after the Battle of Halidon Hill in Scotland and became known as the 'White Knight'.

In 1591 the castle and lands were granted to Sir William Courteney by the Crown, on the condition that he planted English settlers. The castle was retaken by the 'Sugan' Earl in 1598 but the Crown repossessed the castle and lands after some time. In 1638 the properties were regranted to Sir George Courteney. They later were passed on to the Earl of Devon, who was reputed to have been a good landlord.

In 1777, Lord Courtney was in possession of the castle and lands. He is said to have repaired 'one' of the castles for his residence. He is also said to have built a church and a tower.

At Adare Manor museum can be seen some spinctrae or Roman bath tickets from the reign of Tiberius which are impressed with horrible figures. These were dug up at the castle ruins sometime around 1820 by a Mr. Locke.

The fourth Earl of Desmond, who was buried at Askeaton Abbey c. 1399, was known as Gearoid Iarla (the Earl Garrett). He was known to have been a poet and a magician and was reputed to have vanished into the lake of Lough Gur where he lies sleeping with his army and rides over the waves on his horse on a certain night of every seventh year.

Newcastle Castle 2
Parish: Kilmurry / Cill Mhuire – church of Mary
Townland: Newcastle
OS Sheet 65 ref 612 573
Situated about 3 kilometres east from Limerick beside the N7.

This castle stood on a rock in the townland of Newcastle. It was described by Curry in 1840 as being in good condition except for the west wall which had fallen. Measuring about 18.5 by 6.75 metres and about 19 metres in height, the walls were 1.75 metres thick. According to tradition a square tower at the southwest corner had fallen into ruins and the stones had been removed. It appears that this section had five storeys.

It is reputed that, along with Castle Troy, it was built by the Norman family of Troys, de Tryos, or O'Treos, but this is open to question.

Nicker Castle
Parish: Grean / Grian – sun (sunny place)
Townland: Nicker
Barony: Coonagh
OS Sheet 65 ref 762 457
Situated about 2 kilometres southwest of New Pallas Grean.

This castle was situated in the small village of Nicker on a high and rocky outcrop. Nothing remained in 1840. This was a castle of the O'Briens of Coonagh.

See also in this area Kilduff Castle and Ballytrasna Castle.

Oola/Ulla Castle
Parish: Oola / Ulla – apples
Townland: Oola /Oollahills
Barony: Coonagh
OS Sheet 66 ref 836 418

Oola is a name of a village about 4 miles from New Pallasgrean and which is situated just near the Tipperary border. The castle was on the eastern side of Oola hill, not far away from the village.

In the townland of Oola there was a square castle which was in a reasonable state in 1840. It measured about 6.5 metres square and about 18.5 metres in height. Probably, it had five storeys which contained very small chambers. Oola Castle is said to have been built during the reign of Elizabeth but it is more than likely it was built by the White Knight.

Two miles or so away is Dromkeen and further on is Caherconlish. Caherconlish was a walled town in 1358. (Caherconlish / Caathair Chinn Lis – stone fort near the Lis.)

Palacegrean (Pallas Grean) Castle

Parish: Grean / Grian – sun (sunny place)
Townland: Cloghaderreen
Barony: Coonagh
OS Sheet 65 ref 764 436
Situated about 500 metres southeast of the crossroads at Old Pallas Grean.
Pailis Ghreine – Palace or fortress of Graine – the sun goddess – Irish Graine for sun.

There are two villages named Pallas Grean which are about 3 kilometres apart. One is called Old Pallas Grean (now called Old Pallas) and the other Pallas Grean New.

The Norman Fitzgeralds moved into the area c. 1200 and soon had a castle built to protect their interests. This castle was built by Maurice Fitzgerald sometime before 1223 when he received a charter to hold a fair in Pallasgreen. He also built a church and laid out a diamond-shaped fairgreen where the original village expanded. It is said that, in 1810, there were remains of the foundations of a castle near the Moat of Grian, which is situated in the northeast corner of the townland of Cloghaderreen. The moat was about 120 metres in circumference at its base and about 20 metres at its height, which was about 9.5 metres. Others said that a castle stood about 40 metres east of the moat. The large limestone blocks have been entirely removed.

About 5 kilometres south of old Palacegrean, close to the ruined castle on the rock of Ballyneety, is the location where Patrick Sarsfield intercepted and destroyed the siege train laden with guns, cannon, ammunition and supplies heading for the siege of Limerick.

Pallaskenry Castle / Shanpallas Castle
Baile Na Martra Castle
Parish: Russel's Chapel
Townland: Shanpallas / Old Pallice
Barony: Kenry
Pailis Chaonrai – palisaded fortress of Kenry
OS Sheet 65 ref 432 548
The castle remains are situated about 2 kilometres east of Pallaskenry.

Reputed to have been built by the O'Donovans, but later, and for many years, became a Fitzgerald possession. In 1840 what remained of the south wall had fallen to the arch on the ground floor and the remaining walls were in fairly good condition. The base of the castle measured 5.25 by 4.5

metres. The height was about 19 metres and the walls were about 1.75 metres in thickness. The castle was built on a low rock about 2.5 kilometres east of the town of Pallas-Kenry. Due to its size it could only be described as a watchtower. About 4.5 metres east of this castle are the remains of a wall or building which measured 17 by 13 metres. The walls are about 9 metres high and 1.5 metres in thickness. It is not known if this was the remains of a previous castle or not.

It is related that, in 1573, when the Earl of Desmond (Garrett) and his cousin John were released from the Tower of London after being imprisoned for over six years, and after a short imprisonment (house-arrest) in Dublin, they made their way south and regained their castles, including Shan-Pallas.

Port (Portanard) Castle

Parish: Abbeyfeale
Townland: Port
Barony: Connello
OS Sheet 72 ref 102 283
Situated 3 kilometres northwest of the town of Abbeyfeale on the north bank of the river Feale.

This castle is situated close to the minor road that runs along the north bank of the river between Abbeyfeale and Listowel. It commanded the crossing point of the river and is reputed to have been one of the castles of the Geraldines.

The castle measures about 13 metres by 10 metres with walls about 1.8 metres thick. It is said that it was a roughly built castle with no outstanding features.

It is related that, while residing here, Thomas, heir to the earldom of Desmond found himself lost when darkness fell while out hunting. Seeing a light in the distance he went towards the house and asked to stay the night. The house happened to belong to one of his father's tenants, a Mr. McCormac who had an extremely beautiful daughter named Catherine. After some time he married her and all his kindred turned against him, saying that a peasant's daughter could not become the Countess of Desmond. Forced to leave, the pair found their way to France where they lived for the remainder of their lives. The earldom of Desmond passed on to the next in succession.

Abbeyfeale derives its name from the Cistercian Abbey. The river gets its name from Fial, the wife of an ancient chieftain. She happened to be bathing in the river when her husband approached. She didn't recognise him and thought it was a stranger. It is said that she died of fright and shame in her nakedness.

Also related is the story that a lady, who lived in Port Castle in bygone years, had three husbands at the same time. This did not advance family harmony as they were always fighting for her favours and became deadly enemies. Hence, we get the name of Portrinard: Port na d'Tri Namhad – the fort of the three enemies.

Pullagh Castle
Parish: Croom / Croma / Cromedh
Townland: Pullagh
Barony: Coshma
OS Sheet 65 ref 502 372
This castle was situated on a low hill beside the road about 4 kilometres southwest of Croom.

Pallaskenry Castle

O'Donovan described it in 1840 as a castle in utter ruins. No further information is available.

Raheen Castle / Cahervally Castle
Parish: Cahervally
Townland: Raheen
Barony: Clanwilliam
OS Sheet 65 ref 596 495

The bare foundations of this castle are situated about 100 metres west of the old church within the circular rath or Caher which gave the parish its name.

The castle belonged to the O'Caseys and later to the Roches.

See also Lickadoon Castle.

Rath Castle
Parish: Abington
Townland: Rath
Barony: Owneybeg
Os Sheet 65 ref 726 525
3 kilometres south of Moroe village close to the Mulkear River.

I have no information on this castle. The site is indicated on the current maps, and the Monuments Survey of Limerick names it as Rath Castle.

Earlier sources refer to a castle at Cappanouk, which is the townland immediately to the east.

Rathcannon Castle
Parish: Athlacca / An t-Ath Leacach – flaggy ford
Townland: Rathcannon
Barony: Coshma
OS Sheet 65 ref 580 345
The castle is situated on a small hill about 2 kilometres east of Athlacca village.

Within a large walled bawn were an almost square tower and another building. This other building was in ruins but still thatched and occupied c. 1840 by someone who had made a shelter for his poor family. The tower was situated in the northwest corner of the bawn and only lower parts of three walls remained and measured about 11 metres square. Only 9.5 metres of the tower's height remained. The walls were about 1.3 metres thick. The bawn's measurements were some 35 by 40 metres. As the walls were in such a ruinous state it was impossible to establish their original height. Indications are that there were small towers on each corner with some flights of stone stairs accessing the top of the walls.

Some sources (i.e. Fitzgerald) say that the O'Caseys built the castle. Lewis also says that it was built by the O'Caseys in the sixteenth century on the site of an ancient fortress. Other sources mention the Norman De Lacy family, which could be more accurate, as they are credited with building the nearby Athlacca and Tullerboy castles.

Rathgonin Castle
Parish: Kilbroderan
Townland: Unknown

Barony: Lower Connello
OS Sheet 64 ref somewhere in the area of 295 415
Exact position unknown.

Lewis mentions Rathgonin Castle as being in this parish but we have no more information.

Rathkeale Castle
Parish: Rathkeale
Townland: Unknown
Barony: Lower Connello
OS Sheet 64 ref 365 415

This castle was built by the Geraldines. Nothing remains only some low-lying ruins. The town of Rathkeale sprung up around the site of this castle.
Refer to Castle Matrix, which was much better known.

Rathmore Castle
Parish: Cahircorney or Manister
Townland: Rathmore North
Barony: Small County
OS Sheet 65 ref 566 414
Castle is situated about 5 kilometres east of Croom, not far from the ruins of Manister Abbey.

It was described as a square tower house about 22.5 metres in height and strongly built. Incorporated in the structure was a vault at the lower level and a high hall above. There were no signs of outworks visible in 1896. There was a thick end wall containing a latrine at ground level. There were five chambers in total and a much bigger sixth chamber with its wall extending upwards from the main hall.

Rathmore was built by the Earl of Desmond in 1306 on the site of an earlier, possibly Danish, fortification. In 1579, John Fitzgerald, brother to the Earl, had a garrison of Irish and Spaniards here. Following the battle of Monasternenagh the castle fell into the hands of the English forces under Malby. The Earl of Desmond records that 'the English murdered all within the walls and took away spoils and writings'. The Geraldines soon reoccupied the castle until Carew finally took it. After this time it fell into ruins.

See also Glenogra.

Rathnaseer (Rath Na Saor) Castle
Parish: Rathkeale / Rath Gaela
Townland: Rathnaseer
Barony: Connello Lower
OS Sheet 64 ref 375 393
3.5 kilometres south-southeast of Rathkeale.

This old castle was located a few hundred metres to the north of the old church, beside a stream which flows into the river Deel. In 1840 it was in ruins. It was but a small castle or watchtower measuring about 4.5 metres by 3.5 metres. There was an arch over the ground floor. Even though small, its walls were over 2 metres thick and it stood about 11 metres in height.

It is said that it was an outpost of the Earls of Desmond

and is where the 'Sugan Earl' was proclaimed Earl of Desmond by O'Neill.

Rathurd Castle
Parish: St Nicholas
Townland: Rathurde
Barony: Liberties of Limerick
OS Sheet 65 ref 595 540
5 kilometres southeast from Limerick City Centre and 1.5 kilometres east of the R511.

This castle is still in existence. It is situated about 750 metres northwest of Domhnach Mor old church. O'Donovan, in 1840, when the walls stood about 11 metres high, described it as a most remarkable building. It is unusual in that it is a round castle on the exterior but square inside and possibly was constructed by the Knights Templar.

The inside measurements were roughly 6.5 metres square and, at their thickest, the walls would measure about 4 metres.

The first level above ground had a timber floor and the third floor is arched underneath. It is not known if the second floor was arched. There are indications of a fourth storey.

Rawleystown (Raleighstown) Castle
Parish: Cahircorney / Cathair Corne – stone fort of Coirne
Townland: Rawleystown
Barony: Small County

OS Sheet 65 ref 654 427
The ruins of this once imposing castle are situated close to the R514, about 3.5 kilometres northwest of Herbertstown and not far south of Caherelly Castle.

This fortress was built by Thomas Raleigh, uncle of Sir Walter, during the reign of James I. It had a bawn defended at the angles by four small towers.

It was later occupied by the Croker family.

Robertstown Castle
Parish: Robertstown
Townland: Robertstown
Barony: Lower Connello
OS Sheet 64 ref 271 501
Situated not far from Dysert Castle on the opposite side of Robertstown Creek. Close to the N69, east of Foynes.

Very little remains of Robertstown Castle except for a few stumps of walls. No record of it being attacked exists but it probably happened during the Desmond Rebellion.

It appears that originally in the thirteenth century all these lands were first held by an Anglo-Norman by the name of Wall (de Val or de Vaal), who became known as De Wall and then later Wall.

The fortification is supposed to be named after a Robert Gore (or de Gore), who is reputed to have built a fortified structure at this site around the year 1201 and then been in occupation of it until 1230. It is not known when the stone castle was built at this location. From 1298 until 1310 it was occupied by descendants of Gore who were named Margery and Gore. The castle and lands were taken over by the Earls of Desmond and during the Desmond Rebellion of James Fitzmaurice the castle was obliged to surrender after a siege. A few years later, under the Munster Plantation, it was in the possession of an English undertaker by the name of William Trenchard, and in 1606 it became the possession of Sir Richard Wingfield who occupied Dysert Castle and its lands, which were all in close proximity.

Robertstown was in the possession of Richard Stephenson of Dunmoylan, a Royalist, at the time of the Cromwellian Confiscations. All the Stephensons' lands were confiscated and handed over to an adventurer called Sir Thomas Chamberlain.

Rockbarton Castle
Parish: Tullerbracky
Townland: Rockbarton or Caher
Barony: Coshma
OS Sheet 65 in area of 614 397
This castle was located about 3 kilometres west of Lough Gur.

There is a possible castle site in this area. It was alluded to in the field name book, but, even in 1840, none of the local people could pinpoint the exact site, as all the stones had been removed.

Rockstown (Rochestown) Castle
Parish: Fedamore / Fiadh Damair – wood of Damar
Townland: Rockstown
Barony: Clanwilliam

OS Sheet 65 ref 624 464
This castle is situated about 22 kilometres south of Limerick to the west of the R512 and about 300 metres north of the old church beside the minor road between Caherconlish and Fedamore.

The ruins stand on a limestone rock which is about 85 metres in diameter. The walls were in perfect condition in the mid-1800s and stood to a height of about 16 metres. It was a tower house, some four storeys high, and the measurements at its base were 8 metres by 7.5 metres on the inside.

Rockstown Castle was built by the de Burgos or the Burkes of Clanwilliam, who also built the nearby castle of Williamstown and possibly the one at the site later occupied by Ballynagarde House. Lewis says it was erected by the Roche family during the reign of Henry VIII, but this is unlikely.

Ryves Castle

Parish: Ballyscadane
Townland: Ryvescastle
Barony: Costlea
OS sheet 73 ref 749 299
This castle is located about 3 kilometres southeast of Knocklong.

Lewis mentions this place as the residence in 1831 of P. Ryan Esq. and states that the churchyard within the castle demesne contains the Ryan family memorial. Elsewhere in his work, Lewis also associates Ryves Castle with the Lowe family, perhaps at an earlier date than the Ryan connection. More than likely this was a castle mansion of the eighteenth century. Whether there was an older castle at the site is open to question.

Shanid Castle
Parish: Kilmoylan / Kilmoylan – church of St. Moelan
Townland: Shanid Lower
Barony: Lower Connello
OS Sheet 64 ref 243 452
This castle is located about 3 kilometres southwest of Shanagolden.

The name Shanid is derived from the Irish word 'Seanaid', which could mean an assembly or senate.

The castle was built on a line of hill running north and south and could be seen against the skyline from many kilometres away on a clear day. It was built on the lowest hill of the ridge. This conical hill had been formed by manpower, in such a way as to build a circular earthen rampart and fosse around the base, which measured about 200 metres in circumference. The inside mound rose to over 20 metres and was topped by a strong, embattled wall which enclosed an area where the tower house stood. When surveyed in 1896 this wall was found to be 4 metres high and a metre broad and the enclosure had a diameter of around 23 metres.

The castle was not built in the centre but to one side, very close to the wall. This tower house or fortification itself is extremely unusual, as externally it was octagonal while the interior was circular, indicating that it was possibly constructed by the Knights Templar, who had other similar buildings in the Limerick area. (See Rathurd.)

The tower was probably one of the smaller towers in Ireland as the inner circular diameter was no more than 7 metres within walls around 3 metres thick. What still stood in 1896 was about 9 metres high.

Shanid was originally a MacSheehy fortification or fort which was later taken over by the Desmonds and became one of their principal fortresses. 'Shanid a Boo', which became the war cry of the Desmonds, derives from the castle. Sometime before 1215, Thomas, son of Maurice Fitzgerald, built a motte and bailey structure on the site of the original fort. He had been granted the area around Shanid by Hamo de Valoignes c. 1198. Maurice was referred to as Maurice the Invader. He was the son of Gerald, the Castellan of Windsor and Nesta an Ryse, daughter of Ap Ryse, Prince of Wales. He arrived in Ireland with his three sons and first settled in Leinster. One son, William, died young. Another, Gerald, eventually established the Kildare branch of the Geraldines, while the third son, Thomas, stayed with his father and became known as Thomas of Shanid. His son, John Fitzgerald, built a stone structure on the site of the old motte and bailey. John and his son Maurice were both killed by Finghin Mac Carthy at the Battle of Callan in 1261. John became known in history as John of Callan.

After the battle of Callan, Finghin Mac Carthy and his army moved into Kerry and Limerick, destroying or capturing every castle and fortification of the Anglo-Normans, including the castle of Shanid and also the one at Newcastle, but these properties were mostly regained after the death of Finghin Mac Carthy at Ringarone near Kinsale.

John of Callan was succeeded by his grandson, Thomas an Apa (ape). The story is told that Thomas as a baby hap-

Shanid Castle

pened to be in Tralee Castle when word was brought of the deaths of his grandfather and father at Callan. Amidst the consternation John was left unattended by his nurse. Excited and bewildered a pet ape grabbed the young baby out of the crib and carried him upstairs to the battlements. No harm was done to the child and he was later returned safely to his cradle.

During the wars of the Roses in England, the Geraldines moved to Askeaton and made that their principal stronghold while a garrison remained at Shanid. During the Desmond Rebellion, the castle at Shanid surrendered after a short siege. Following the end of the second Desmond Rebellion, Shanid ceased to be a Desmond stronghold but it still remained garrisoned by a small Irish force. After destroying or capturing the other Desmond castles in 1600, Sir George Carew decided to march on to Shanid. When the small garrison saw the army approaching they abandoned the castle and Carew moved on, leaving a small garrison at the castle. Red Hugh O'Donnell, on his way to Kinsale in 1601, recaptured the castle but it was again taken by the English and then retaken by the Irish who destroyed most of it with gunpowder in 1641, thus depriving the English of its capture and use once again.

Note: In 1573, the Earl of Desmond put James Dore at the head of all carpenters and also of the masons in his domain, ordering them to raze the castles of Castletown in Kenry and all the castles of the Knights of Glin. During a minor war between the Earls of Desmond and the Butlers, Earls of Ormond, the Earl of Desmond was besieged at Shanid, which at that time was impregnable. However, the Earl's harper opened one of the large doors on the condition that he would be raised higher than his master. Having gained the castle, the Earl of Ormond honoured his pledge by hanging the harper from the highest battlement of the castle while the Earl of Desmond was held prisoner in the main hall.

Skehacreggaun Castle
Parish: Mungret
Townland: Skehacreggaun
Barony: Pubblebrien
OS Sheet 65 ref 538 544

Little is known about this castle which is situated on the south side of the main road opposite Castlemungret. Some lower parts of the walls still exist today.

It is recorded that one J. Scoler held the lands around the castle. In 1656 the lands were in the possession of a Nicholas Stritch.

Skool (School) Castle
Parish: Fedamore / Faidh Damair – wood of Damar
Townland: Skool / School
Barony: Small County
OS Sheet 65 ref 619 442
About 2.5 kilometres east of Fedamore and 1.25 kilometres northwest of the R 512 at Grange.

Very little of this building remains, except for 3 metres of the north wall and 6 metres of the south wall.

It was also called Scule Castle in olden times. There is no further history available.

See also nearby Castlequarter (Fedamore), Rockstown and Williamstown.

Stephenson (Stephenstown) Castle
Parish: Athnassey
Townland: Stephenstown
Barony: Costlea
OS sheet 65 in the area of ref 677 308
This castle was reputed to have been located approximately 4 kilometres west of Knocklong and not far from Elton.

Lewis mentions a possible castle site at 'Stephenson' in this parish. No further information available.

Stoneville Castle
Parish: Nantenan / Naenntenan – land of nettles
Townland: Stoneville
Barony: Lower Connello
OS Sheet 64 ref 355 440
The exact position of Stoneville Castle is not clear but it was supposed to be situated about 4 kilometres north from Rathkeale to the west of the R518.

All that Curry said was that the ruins of a castle stood beside a mansion called 'Stoneville House', which was the same name as the old castle. Other references give the mansion the name of Stonepark House.

Tankerdstown Castle

Parish: Tankerdstown / Baile Thancaird – Tacred's townland
Townland: Tankardstown North
Barony: Coshma?
OS Sheet 73 ref 575 289

Ruins of this castle are situated about 3 kilometres northwest of Kilmallock, not far from the walled town of Kilmallock and some 2 kilometres southeast of Bruree.

A part of the castle was standing in 1828 but traces of the structure were gone when John O'Donovan visited the location in 1840. He was informed by some old people of the exact site and that it was known as 'Caislean Bhaile an Airighthe'. More than likely the name takes its origin from a Norman family called Tacred or Tankard. Some sources say that the Tankard name was of Flemish or German origin, from those who settled around Southern Wales.

It appears that Anne, the widow of John De Cogan of Cork, claimed the dower of Tankerstown from De Lees and de Goulys c. 1272 but in 1291 they still remained in possession. A Gerald Tankard tried to repossess Tankerdstown for John de Penrys sometime later but failed in his attempt. In the early 1300s we find that a Russell family were in occupation. These must have been relations of the Tankards as they are mentioned as Tankard Russells. Also, we find mention of a Walter Russel of Bruree and a Thomas Russell of Knocksouna.

The parish of Tankerdstown consisted of Ballygubba, Knocksouna (Cnoc Samhna) and Tankerdstown. As a result of the Cromwellian Plantation, the above townlands, which were in the ownership of Ellen Lacy (née Fitzgerald), were acquired by Captain Charles Ormsby in trust for his son.

The Ormsby family was still in ownership up to 1805. Others of this same Ormsby family, including Arthur and Charles, acquired vast tracts of land in the nearby parishes, including Athlacca. One of these was known to be a vicious and ruthless landowner. To acquire these vast tracts of good land they must have bought out the interests of the other Cromwellian soldiers who had been granted lands in that area.

See also Ballygubba.

Also, Ballysiward (Howardstown) belonging to the Norman family Dundons, Ballyhinnaught, Knocksouna and Clogher East. These must have been all De Lacy castles as they are in such close proximity to one another – one in nearly every townland!

Thomastown Castle
Parish: Unknown
Townland: Thomastown
OS Sheet 73 ref 565 255
This castle was supposed to have existed about 5 kilometres southwest of Kilmallock.

Tomdeely Castle
Parish: Toomdeely / Tom Dhaoile – bush on the River Deel
Townland: Tomdeely
Barony: Shanid division of Connello
OS Sheet 64 ref 324 519
This castle was situated on low land close to the Shannon 2.5 kilometres northwest of Askeaton

Irish = Tum Daoile – bush of the river Deel or the tumulus at the river Deel?

The land around the castle is mentioned as being in the possession of a Myler Fitzhenry in 1201. The construction date of the castle is unknown but in 1223 it became the residence of Bishop Hubert de Burgo of Limerick and was referred to as the Bishop's palace. In 1251 Bishop Robert of Limerick granted the lands of Toomdeely to the widow of Tyrell de Kardyff (Tyrell of Cardiff) but it again reverted to the Bishop of Limerick in 1336. There is no record of it ever being attacked.

Sometime later and before 1580 it became part of the Desmond estate under Thomas Cam Fitzgerald and Edmond Óg Lacy was in possession. Soon afterwards, he was killed in the church of Knockpatrick for his part in the Desmond Rebellion. De Lacy's property was then granted to the Elizabethan undertaker William Trenchard. Later, the castle was occupied by a Nicholas Lillis, who rented it from Trenchard. Again it changed hands after the Desmond Rebellion when it was granted to the widow of Bishop Gaugh, who never occupied the castle, and sometime later it was granted to Francis Berkely of Askeaton, who later passed it on to his son. After the Berkley occupation it reverted to the Protestant Bishop of Limerick. From 1655 the castle and lands were in the possession of Lord Broghill, the Earl of Cork. The castle was almost in ruins at this time and unfit for occupation.

Some distance from the castle are the ruins of a rectangular castle-like house measuring about 23 metres by 13 metres. Probably a later castellated house, it is not known who built this house or who occupied it.

Tooreen Castle

Parish: Carrigparson / Carraig a' Phaearsuin – rock of the parish priest?
Townland: Tooreen
OS Sheet 65 ref area of 632 534
Castle ruins are situated about 7 kilometres southeast of Limerick.

This parish was called after a rocky hill to the west of an old church called Carrigperson. It is not known how the area got its name or who was the priest or parson. Only parts of the walls remained in 1840. These consisted of 6 metres of the north wall and about 2.5 metres of the east and the west walls. The castle measured just over 6.5 metres from east to west but the dimensions of the south wall could not be measured. No further details could be ascertained.
    See also Cahernarry.

Tullabracky Castle

Parish: Tullabracky
Townland: Tullabracky Bishopland
Barony: Coshma / Small County
OS Sheet 65 ref 623 382
2 kilometres north of Bruff west of the R 512.

This castle was in the vicinity of the Holy Well south of the old church.
    The site was levelled around 1810 by the Maloney family, who built a farmhouse using part of the lower walls for an outhouse.

Tullerboy Castle / Castle Ivers
Parish: Athlacca
Townland: Tullerboy
Barony: Coshma
OS Sheet 65 ref 555 362

This was a DeLacey Castle situated about 2 kilometres north of Athlacca village where that family also had a castle. Castle Ivers is a later house, built adjoining the ruins of Tullerboy Castle.

Tullovin Castle
Parish: Croom / Croma / Cromedh
Townland: Tullovin
OS Sheet 65 ref 536 388
Castle situated on the east side of Tullovin Hill 4.5 kilometres southeast of Croom.

There are ruins of a fair-sized castle with a 'Sheela-na Gig' in the wall. This castle has been referred to as the Palace of Carrigparson although this seems doubtful as Carrigparson parish is up by Limerick.
   See also Tooreen Castle.

Williamstown Castle
Parish: Fedamore / Fiadh Damair – wood of Damar
Townland: Williamstown
Barony: Clanwilliam
OS Sheet 65 ref 614 470

The ruins are situated only a couple of kilometres from Rockstown Castle.

Part of the ruins of this tower house can still be seen today. It was a plain, almost square, building devoid of any fortifications or outworks. Originally it belonged to the de Burgos or Burkes and later passed on to the Crokers. The Crokers repaired the castle when they came into occupation.

About 3 kilometres to the north is the Hill of Knockhay or Knockea where a strong fortification existed. Little is known about its exact purpose, size and history. There are remains of a square and a round building encircled by a deep dry fosse with a rampart of earth and stone. Maybe, this was an old Irish fort where the Anglo-Normans or the de Burgo family built their original fortification.

Woodstock Castle / Bonistoe Castle
Parish: Ballingarry
Townland: Woodstock
Barony: Upper Connello
OS Sheet 65 ref 419 373
Woodstock Castle (Bun a Stoigh) was situated about 1.25 kilometres northeast from the town of Ballingarry, just to the west of the Adare road.

The castle measured about twenty 6.8 metres by 4.75 metres on the outside and the walls were almost 2 metres in thickness. When examined for the Ordnance Survey around 1840 the walls stood 11 metres high. Woodstock was described at that time as a very old castle or tower house but its history was unknown.

There were two monasteries nearby – Kilshane, and a Cistercian Abbey, which have disappeared from the landscape. Both were erected by the Fitzgeralds of Clonlish. Probably the Fitzgeralds also built this particular castle.

A religious house called the Priory was located not far away. The field where some of the foundations have been found is called the 'Friary Field'. It is said that this priory belonged to the Knights Bannerets. Nearby in the same townland is situated a bastion or turret of an old castle said to have been occupied by the De Lacy family. It is known locally as 'the Turret'.

Index of alternative names

Abbeyfeale – see Port Castle
Baille na Matra – see Pallaskenry
Ballinaveala – see Crecora
Ballyneety – see Longford
Bonistoe – see Woodstock
Butler's – see Abington
Cahervally – see Raheen
Carrigfariogla – see Carrigareely
Carrigonan – see Carrickania
Castle Egney – see Ballyegan
Castle English – see Cleanlis
Castle Hewson – see Ballyengland
Castle Ivers – see Tullerboy
Castle Roe – see Newcastle 1
Doon Castle, Lough Gur – see Bouchier's
Fanning's Castle – see Whitmore's
Howardstown – see Ballysiward
Kenmare – see Hospital
Kilbigly – see Brickfield
Kilcolman – see Kilbehenny
Killalough – see Black Castle, Lough Gur
Knocknagaul – see Ballyclogh 1
Lotteragh – see Bruree
Mac Eineiry – see Castletown 1
Mahoonagh – see Castlemahon
Meine Castle – see Castlemahon
O'Farrell's rock – see Carrigareely
Old Court Castle – see Ballybricken
Rathsiward – see Castle Siward
Rochestown – see Rockstown
Shanpallas – see Pallaskenry

Springfield – see Gurtnetubber
Tobernea – see Leagaun
Woney – see Abington
Woodfort – see Lisnacullia

In most cases I have not listed Irish spellings of a well-known English name. Nor have I listed the many variant spellings or very similar alternate names where common sense should suffice to find the correct entry. The list is predominantly of those alternate names which are sufficiently different to be a source of confusion.

Bibliography

O'Donovan, John etc.; Ordnance Survey Letters, County Limerick (1840).

Lewis, Samuel; *Topographical Dictionary of Ireland* (London, 1837).

Westropp, Thomas John; *The Ancient Castles of County Limerick* (1906) Lenihan, Maurice; *Limerick, Its History and Antiquities* (Dublin, 1866).

Dowd, James; *The County of Limerick* (Limerick, 1896).

Spellissy, Sean; *The History of Limerick City* (Celtic Bookshop, 1998).

Seoighe, Mainchin; *Portrait of Limerick* (London, 1982).

Seoighe, Mainchin; *From Bruree to Corcomohide* (Bruree, Ireland, 2000).

Culhane, Thomas J; *The Barony of Shanid* (Mount Pleasant, Ireland, 2003).

Carroll, Joe & Tuohy, Pat; *Village By Shannon* (Limerick, 1991).

Cronin, Patrick J; *Eas Céad Tine* (Askeaton, Ireland, 1999).

O'Connor, John; *On Shannon's Shore* (Pubblebrien Hist. Soc., 2003).

Salter, Mike; *Castles and Stronghouses of Ireland* (Folly, UK, 1993).

Nicholson, Helen; *The Knights Templar* (Sutton, UK, 2001).

Ordnance Survey of Ireland discovery series, sheets 58, 64, 65, 66, 72, 73.

Also available by the same author

The Castles and Fortified Houses of West Cork
ISBN 0 95194158 5

An indispensable reference to the history of West Cork from 1150 to 1700 with details of the history and legends surrounding the castles With individual entries for 110 castles, line drawings by Martin Law and map.

The Castles of The Kingdom of Kerry
ISBN 0 95194155 0

A glimpse into the history of Kerry and Desmond between 1190 and 1700. A substantial historical introduction is followed by over 100 entries, accompanied by colour photographs, black and white drawings and maps.

A Bay of Destiny
Where the Deer Ran Wild
March Into Oblivion
Sive O'Leary